OWL

Greey de Pencier Books

WINTER FUN

Edited by Laima Dingwall and Annabel Slaight

WINTER FUN

OWL Books are published in Canada by Greey de Pencier Books, Toronto. OWL is a trademark of the Young Naturalist Foundation.

©1987, Greey de Pencier Books. First published as THE WINTER FUN BOOK, ©1980. No part of this book may be reproduced or copied in any form without written permission from the publisher.

Published simultaneously in the United States in 1992 by Firefly Books (U.S.) Inc., P.O. Box 1338, Ellicott Station, Buffalo, NY 14205

Printed in Hong Kong

Canadian Cataloguing in Publication Data
Main entry under title:

Winter fun

First published, 1980, under title:
The Winter fun book. Reprinted, 1983, under title: Owl's winter fun.
ISBN 0-919872-86-7

1. Amusements – Juvenile literature.
2. Winter – Juvenile literature. I. Dingwall, Laima, 1953- . II. Slaight, Annabel, 1940- . III. Title: Owl's winter fun.

GV1203.W56 1987   790.I'922   C87-093419-08

Acknowledgements:
Design Director Nick Milton
Designer Diana Glennie
Cover illustration by Lynda Cooper
Special thanks to Mary Anne Brinckman and Sylvia Funston

CONTENTS

A BOOK FULL OF WINTER FUN

What's special about winter for you? Everyone looks forward to different things—building big snowmen, skating or skiing, tramping through the frozen woodlands or curling up by a crackling fire with a warm mug of chocolate. Now there's a book full of terrific ideas for winter fun that makes you say hooray for winter too. Here it is—OWL's Winter Fun book. In it are as many things as we could think of to help you make the very most of winter this year and for many others to come.

Ever wonder what winter is like in other parts of

THIS BOOK IS GREAT. IT TELLS YOU METRIC MEASUREMENTS.

AND FEET AND INCHES TOO!

the world, or out of this world on a planet like Mars? You'll find out right here. You'll also discover why penguins' feet don't get cold, what it's like to hibernate, why it's so quiet after a snowfall, and even why we have winter at all.

But that's only the beginning. There are stories and comics to read, puzzles to do, jokes to share, plants to grow, yummy things to cook, games to play, science projects to experiment with, not to mention all sorts of neat things to think about and astound your friends with.

This book is guaranteed to make winter a great event for you. Turn the page and let the fun begin.

IT ALL DEPENDS WHERE YOU'RE AT!

The next time you dash out of the house looking for frosty winter fun, you can be sure that someone in another part of the world is dashing into the ocean trying to cool off. True! Take the quick tour here, and you'll see for yourself. (If you start feeling topsy-turvy, look at the chart showing the starting dates of the seasons north and south of the Equator.)

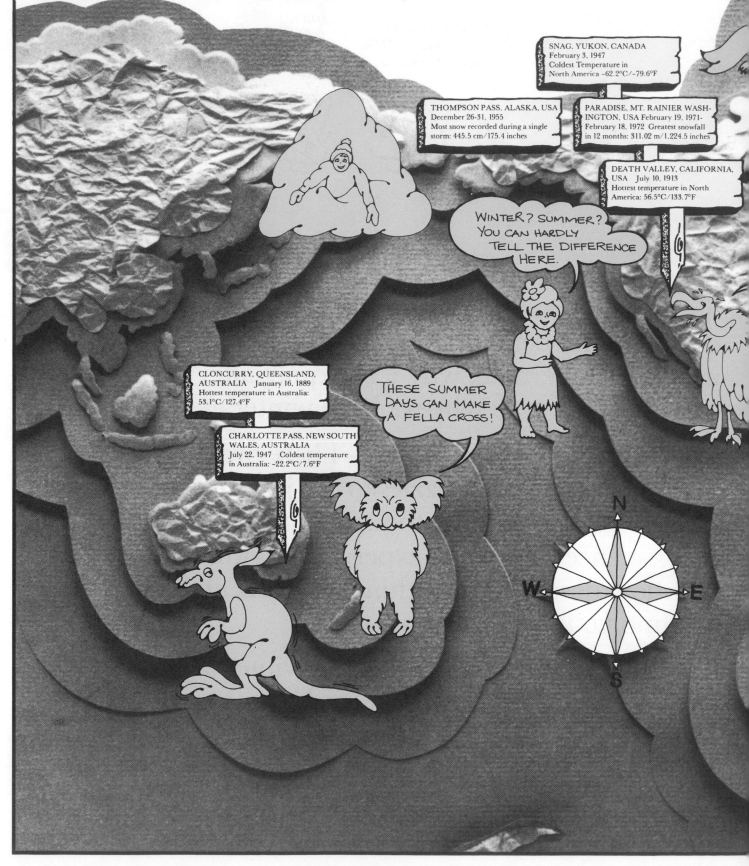

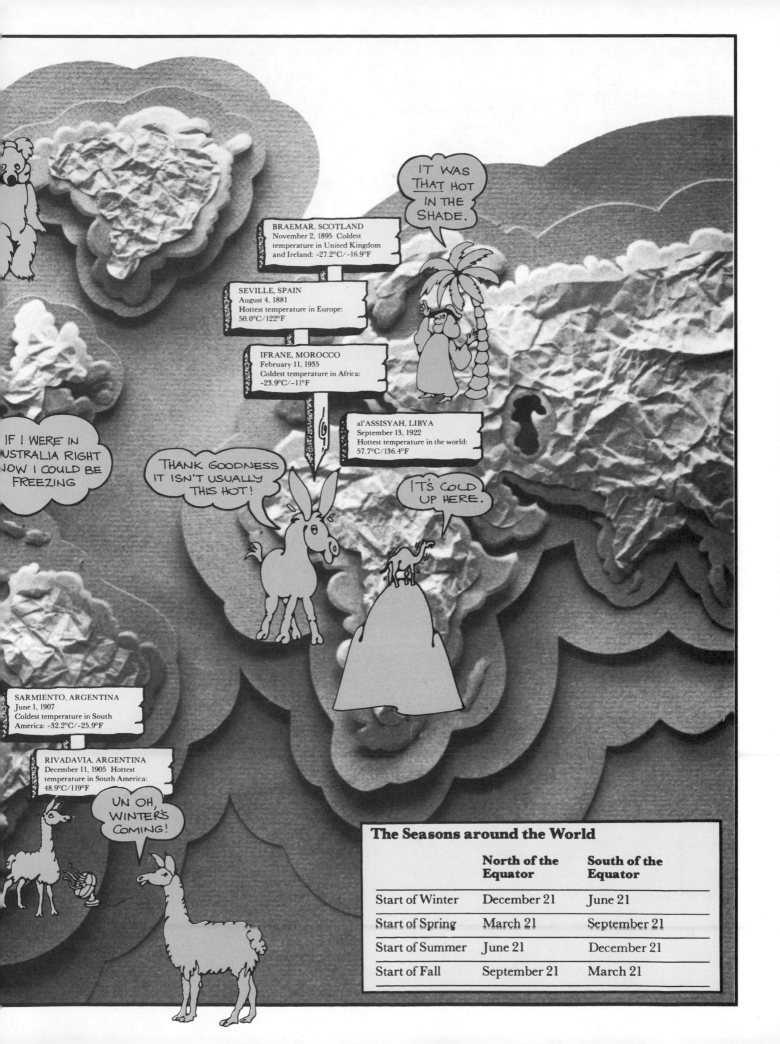

The Seasons around the World

	North of the Equator	South of the Equator
Start of Winter	December 21	June 21
Start of Spring	March 21	September 21
Start of Summer	June 21	December 21
Start of Fall	September 21	March 21

How to Make Winter With an Apple

While you are reading this, several things are happening to the earth.

First, every 24 hours our planet spins once around on an imaginary stick that's tilted. In addition to this spinning, earth is also traveling through space on a path around the sun. The complete trip takes one year and is what makes the seasons happen.

An apple (for earth), a lamp (for the sun) and a stick or knitting needle are all you need to see what happens as earth travels around the sun. Get ready for this experiment by piercing the apple with the

stick or knitting needle and then holding the apple at a tilt.

Now move the tilted apple around the lamp and you will see how seasons happen. When there is a light shining on the apple's stem, it is summer on the top half of the apple. (The less distance the rays from the lamp have to travel, the stronger, and warmer, they are.) As you continue to move the tilted apple around the lamp, the top half of the apple will become shaded and it will be summer on the bottom half of the apple and winter on the top half. The middle of the apple stays closest to the lamp, hence the steady heat all year round at the equator.

10

FOOLING MOTHER NATURE

Many bulbs such as tulips, daffodils, hyacinths and crocuses can be fooled into blooming in the winter. It takes a lot of time, but the results are well worth the effort.

You'll need:
- firm-feeling bulbs (you can buy special varieties for "forcing," which means growing indoors in the winter)
- pots with drainage holes in the bottom
- small, flattish stones or pieces of broken crockery
- potting soil mixed with one-third sand, one-third peat or vermiculite (you can buy all these in any garden or hardware store)
- a dark, cold place to store your bulbs
- newspapers

Getting Started
1. Soak new clay pots overnight before using them; otherwise, the clay will draw water out of the soil and you'll end up with thirsty bulbs.

2. Place the small stones or broken crockery in the bottom of the pots so the earth won't clog the drainage holes.

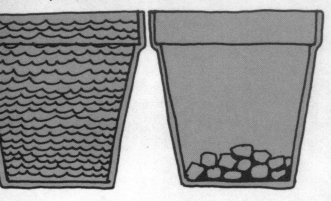

3. Fill the pots with soil and plant the bulbs so their pointed ends are 2.5 cm/1 inch above the surface. Don't let the bulbs touch each other.

4. Water thoroughly.

5. If you like, label each pot with the name and color of the bulbs, and the date of planting.

TULIPS. 24/2/81

Helping Your Bulbs Grow

Find a cold place to keep your bulbs. A garage or unheated basement is perfect, as long as the temperature is above freezing. Your bulbs must be kept in the dark, so if your cold place is light, cover the pots with newspapers.

Keep the soil moist for 10-12 weeks by watering every few days.

When the bulbs have strong roots and the leaves have sprouted up to 9 cm/3.5 inches (5 cm/2 inches for crocuses), it's time to bring them into a cool part of the house. Remember, they've been in a cold, dark place for a long time so they shouldn't have too much heat or light at first.

After a few days you can proudly bring your bulbs into your living room. Soon they'll bloom beautifully—just don't forget to continue watering them.

And now for a sneak preview...
What's happening inside those bulbs, you wonder? Since you probably won't want to cut any of yours apart, have a look below. You can see that there's a miniature flower inside, (it's a hyacinth) just waiting for some moisture so it can start growing.

Super Easy, Speedy Bulbs

Narcissi (also called paper whites) grow much faster than other bulbs. And it's very easy to grow them.

1. Put the bulbs in a shallow dish in a window and almost cover them with small stones. (If you can't find stones, sand or earth will do.)

2. Pour water into the dish until the stones are just covered.

3. Keep the water level up and watch what happens.

ANY WAY YOU SAY IT!

Whatever snowy place in the world you go, everyone says the same thing when the first flurries of the year fly: "It's snowing!!" Do you think you could understand?

Kar yaǵıyor!
(Turkish: *say it* car yah e your)

Il neige!
(French: *say it* eel nayzhe)

تثلج السماء
(Arabic: *say it* tooth ledge assama a)

(Inuit: *say it* kannerpok)

Está nevando!
(Spanish: *say it* esta ne van do)

Det sneer!
(Danish: *say it* de snayer)

बरफ़ पड़ रही है
(Hindi: *say it* baraf gerti)

Está a nevar!
(Portugueese: *say it* esh ta na var)

Het sneeuwt!
(Dutch: *say it* het snayoot)

(Cree: *say it* mi spoon)

ゆきがふります。
(Japanese: *say it* yuki ga furi masu)

Special thanks to the Metropolitan Toronto Library Languages Centre for their help.

HOORAY FOR SNOW!

Snow! It's just tiny droplets of water frozen into crystals that join together and fall from the clouds to the Earth. But add a little sunshine and blue sky, and snow becomes much more than that. It's a soft white blanket that turns the world into an adventureland.

17

Snow can be a monster . . .

Or a crazy battle ground to play in.

Snow is a magical slide to ride . . .

It lets you make shadowy footprint puzzles to solve . . .

Fun, isn't it?

DR. ZED'S SUPER-SQUINT SUN-SHADES

To make your anti-glare goggles you'll need:
heavy cardboard 15 cm by 5 cm/6 inches by 2 inches
ruler
pencil
scissors
two pieces of string, each ½ m/1½ feet long
pencils or crayons

1. Hold the cardboard up to your face so a friend can mark the spots for your eyes.

2. Using a pencil and a ruler draw two small slits.

3. Cut out the slits with scissors.

4. Make a notch for your nose.

5. Poke a hole in either side of the goggles, loop a string through each hole and tie it. Color your goggles with your own design and they're ready to wear.

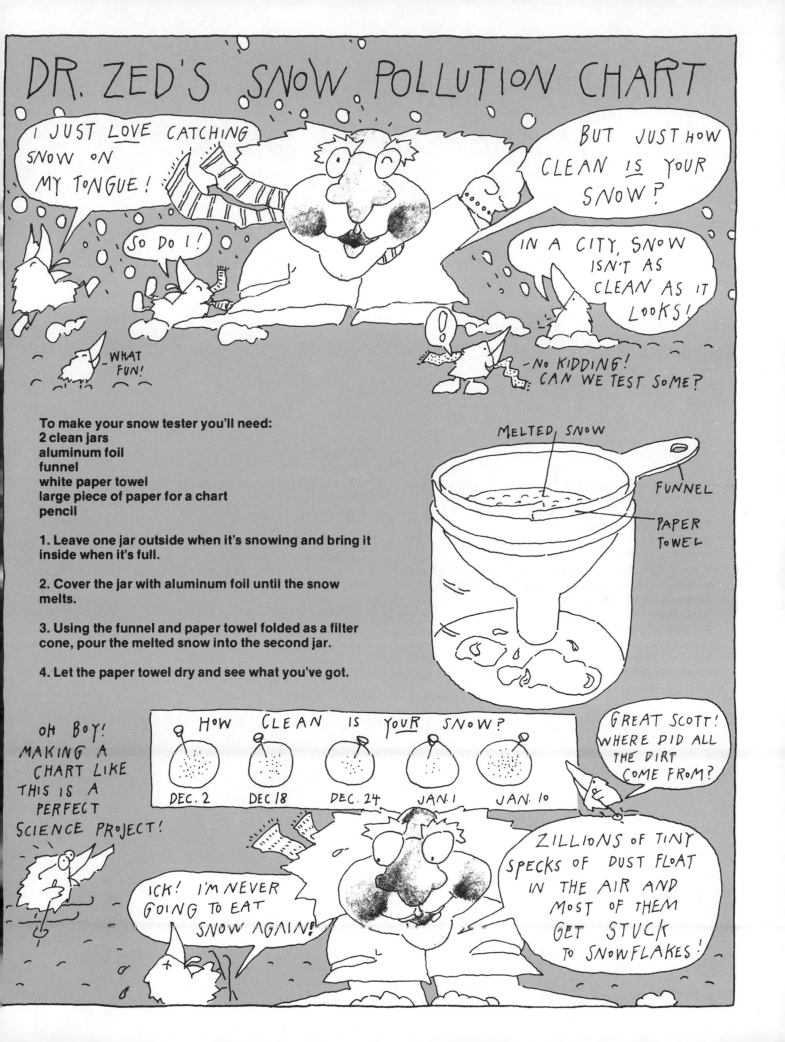

To make your snow tester you'll need:
2 clean jars
aluminum foil
funnel
white paper towel
large piece of paper for a chart
pencil

1. Leave one jar outside when it's snowing and bring it inside when it's full.

2. Cover the jar with aluminum foil until the snow melts.

3. Using the funnel and paper towel folded as a filter cone, pour the melted snow into the second jar.

4. Let the paper towel dry and see what you've got.

DR. ZED'S TERRIFIC TEMPERATURE-TAKER FOR SNOW!

To make your own snow thermometer, you'll need:
outdoor thermometer
long stick or pole (a broom handle works best)
masking tape
watch

1. Tape an outdoor thermometer to the end of a pole, making sure that you don't cover the bulb with tape. Presto—a snow thermometer.

2. Gently push your pole into a snowdrift, thermometer-end first.

3. Leave the thermometer in the snow for five minutes, then take it out and read the temperature.

4. Take snow temperatures in different places—try under trees, in shallow snow and deep snow and wherever else you want.

5. After taking each snow temperature, take the air temperature by sticking your pole into a snowbank so the thermometer points up. Wait five minutes before reading it.

6. Make a chart to compare the different snow and air temperatures.

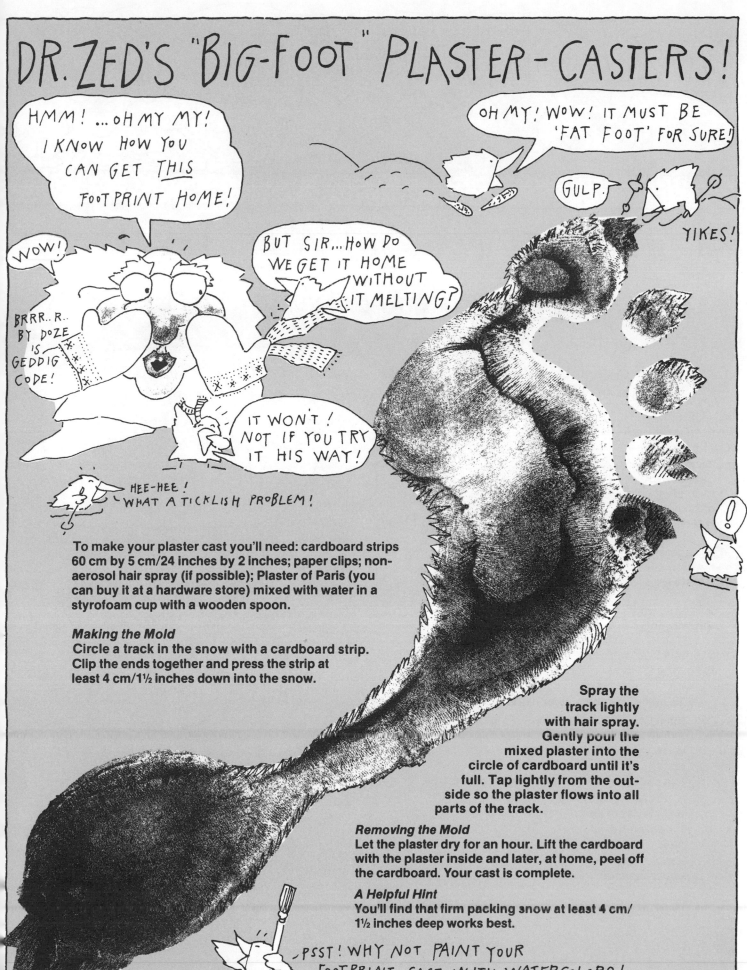

DR. ZED'S "BIG-FOOT" PLASTER-CASTERS!

To make your plaster cast you'll need: cardboard strips 60 cm by 5 cm/24 inches by 2 inches; paper clips; non-aerosol hair spray (if possible); Plaster of Paris (you can buy it at a hardware store) mixed with water in a styrofoam cup with a wooden spoon.

Making the Mold
Circle a track in the snow with a cardboard strip. Clip the ends together and press the strip at least 4 cm/1½ inches down into the snow.

Spray the track lightly with hair spray. Gently pour the mixed plaster into the circle of cardboard until it's full. Tap lightly from the outside so the plaster flows into all parts of the track.

Removing the Mold
Let the plaster dry for an hour. Lift the cardboard with the plaster inside and later, at home, peel off the cardboard. Your cast is complete.

A Helpful Hint
You'll find that firm packing snow at least 4 cm/1½ inches deep works best.

BUT...IT SOUNDS COMPLICATED!

NOT WITH A HANDY MINI-SOLAR HEATER!

GLINT.

SHINE

SHINE

1. **Carefully copy the pattern above onto thick cardboard. Cut out.**

2. **Trace the thick cardboard shape onto the 10 pieces of thin cardboard. Cut each out.**

3. **Now trace the shape 10 times onto aluminum foil and cut out. Glue one piece of foil—shiny side up—to the back of each piece of thin cardboard.**

4. **Carefully punch a hole through each shape where shown.**

5. **Stack the shapes in a pile—shiny side up—and poke a paper fastener through all 10, and fasten.**

6. **Spread the shapes out in a circle and connect the notches so they join like a fan. Your heater is almost ready.**

7. **Slightly curve the shapes upward so your heater looks like a small bowl. Take it out in the sun.**

PAPER FASTENER

HOORAY FOR SUN COLLECTING!

I'M GETTING A SUNTAN!

BOOK ON SOLAR HEATERS

TOAST TOAST

AMAZING! SOME LARGE SOLAR HEATERS CAN GET AS HOT AS 2000°C! ...HOT ENOUGH TO MELT HUGE BLOCKS OF IRON!

RIGHT! BUT THIS SOLAR HEATER IS SO SMALL... IT WON'T HURT YOU... IT WILL JUST WARM YOUR HANDS!

OWL's Winter Fun Crossword Puzzle

This crossword puzzle is about things you can see and do in winter. All the clues and words are found somewhere in this book. The words marked * also have picture clues to help you.

Answers on page 128

Across

1. Tie a _ _ _ _ _ around your neck to keep warm on chilly days. *
4. The Arctic ground squirrel takes a _ _ _ that lasts all winter.
6. The Mighty _ _ _ _ _ have a winter adventure with an otter. *
9. The Mites ride underwater with an _ _ _ _ _ (see 6 across)*
10. It's always cooler on top of a mountain because there's less _ _ _ to be warmed by the sun's rays.
11. We wish you a _ _ _ _ _ Christmas.
13. In olde tyme winters people travelled from place to place in horse-drawn _ _ _ _ _. *
16. Hockey star Frank Mahovlich shares some of his _ _ _ _ _ _ _ _ _ _ with you so you can play better.
18. The opposite of lose.
20. A fierce snowstorm that rhymes with lizard.
22. An animal's footprints in the snow. *
24. Put another log on the _ _ _ _.
25. A bird's home.
27. The Saint Bernard is a search _ _ _ _ _ _ dog. *
29. The vole builds _ _ _ _ _ _ _ through the snow.

30. When it's winter in Canada, it's _ _ _ _ _ _ in Australia.

Down

1. If it doesn't _ _ _ _, you can't ski.
2. The coldest area in the world.
3. _ _ _ _ animals live in barns in the winter.
4. Opposite of far.
5. Dress warmly before you go out and _ _ _ _ in the snow.
6. Winter on _ _ _ _ is twice as cold and twice as long as it is on Earth. *
7. An old-fashioned spelling for "time".
8. A bird _ _ _ _ on its eggs to hatch them.

12. Rudolph, the red-nosed _ _ _ _ _ _ _.
14. Opposite of high.
15. Bears hibernate in a _ _ _ all winter.
16. What bears do in winter. (See 15 down)
17. You need _ _ _ _ _ _ to play ice hockey. *
19. There's _ _ _ _ _ _ _ in the middle of Baked Alaska.
21. _ _ _ _ _ _ _ adapt to winter in amazing ways.
23. Are you a cross-country _ _ _ _ _ ?
26. Some Eskimos' summer home.
28. The Montreal Canadiens is a hockey _ _ _ _.

29

SNOW SLEUTH QUIZ

Here's a quiz which will help you become a super snow sleuth. Read the questions, look carefully at the clues and try to work out what has happened. Good luck, have fun and try it in your neighborhood!
Answers on page 128.

1. If it is warm enough to melt the snow, how was it cold enough for the water to freeze into icicles?

2. Why has the snow melted off the roof of this house but left a rim of snow around the edge?

3. Is this a snow lamb?

4. There are two driveways in this picture: which one was cleared with a plow and which one with a snow blower?

5. Why are these icicles crooked?

6. Why is there no snow on the manhole cover?

7. What made these tracks?

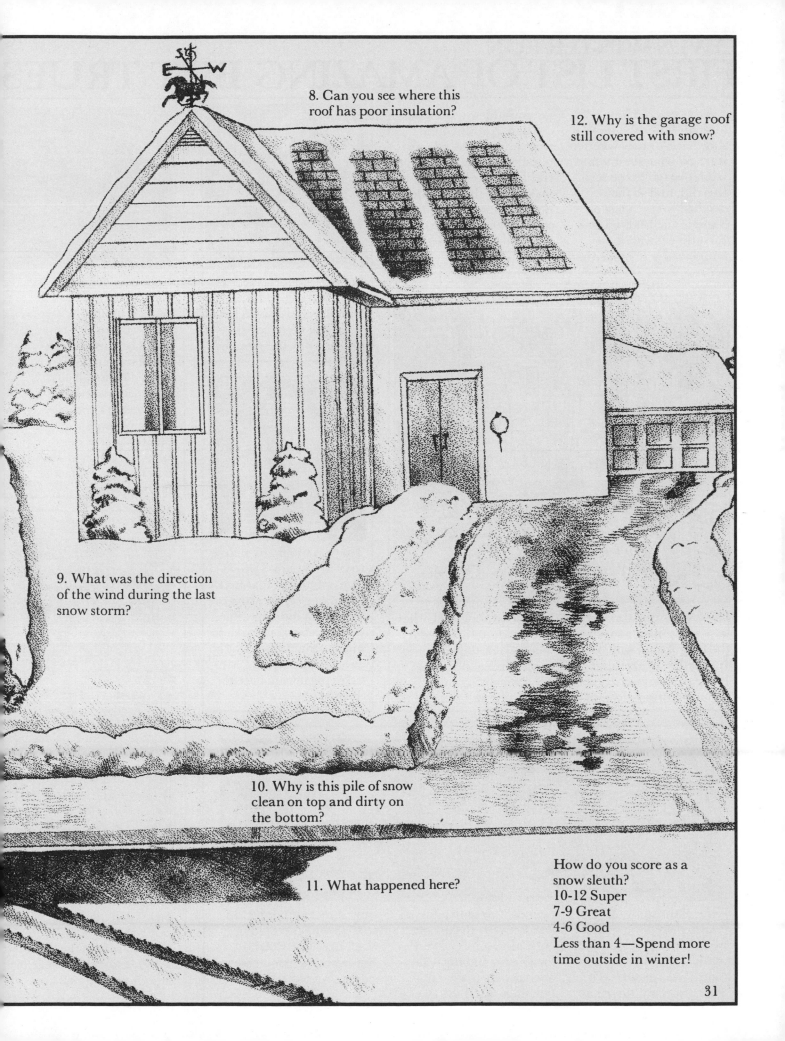

8. Can you see where this roof has poor insulation?

12. Why is the garage roof still covered with snow?

9. What was the direction of the wind during the last snow storm?

10. Why is this pile of snow clean on top and dirty on the bottom?

11. What happened here?

How do you score as a snow sleuth?
10-12 Super
7-9 Great
4-6 Good
Less than 4—Spend more time outside in winter!

Ever wondered how animals—like the snow-shoe hare—know when to start growing their white winter coats? Some scientists did, and so they decided to run a test on hares in their laboratory. First they lowered the temperature to make the animals think winter was coming. Nothing happened. Next, the scientists blindfolded the hares several hours each day to make them think the days were getting shorter. Sure enough, the hares' coats changed from brown to white.

In parts of Siberia it gets so cold that if you pour boiling water from a kettle, it will turn to ice before it hits the ground.

A penguin doesn't worry about cold feet as it stands around on an ice floe. That's because the bottom of its feet are covered by tough cold-proof pads called *papillae*. When it's very cold, a penguin will sometimes rock right back on its tail feathers so its feet don't touch the ice at all.

FILL'ER UP. AND CLEAN THE WINDOWS

Have you ever wondered how some insects survive the long Arctic winter? Just before freeze-up they stop eating and start making and storing glycerol (a type of alcohol) and other chemicals in their body. These work the same way as anti-freeze does in a car, preventing them from freezing.

There are so many maple trees in Canada's province of Quebec that making maple syrup is a very important industry. Each year Quebeckers make so much syrup that it would cover eight stacks of pancakes piled from here to the moon!

NOW THAT'S AN ICECUBE MY DEAR!

About 15,000 large icebergs break loose every year along the shores of Greenland. Some towers are as high above the water as a 30-story building (that means they're 60 stories below the water) and are as long as 2 km/1.2 miles.

LOOKS LIKE A VERY COLD WINTER!

TUG A DUCK CONTEST

One of the most unusual ways of predicting future weather comes from the natives who live in the north. As legend has it, every autumn these natives used to hold a tug-of-war between the people born in summer (called the Ducks) and the winter-born people (called the Ptarmigans). If the Ducks won, it meant that the upcoming winter would be mild, but if the Ptarmigans won, the winter was sure to be cold.

One snowflake may not weigh much, but a 25 cm/10 inch snowfall over an area the size of a city block weighs about the same as 18 full-grown African elephants. Think of that the next time you're shovelling the driveway.

When Canadian mechanical whiz L. Armand Bombardier invented a machine called the snowmobile in 1922, people couldn't stop laughing. The contraption looked so funny because it was an airplane propellor on the front of an old car that had skis instead of wheels. Who would have thought that today his machine would be used to round up reindeer herds, lay down pipelines and drag heavy logs, not to mention just going for a happy ride in the snow?

No wonder the Saint Bernard is the most famous rescue dog in history. It will not only find survivors under deep snow but it will help dig them out and then lie next to them to keep them warm.

Trees growing sideways? It happens in Canada's Northwest Territories, where black spruce are forced to grow horizontally along the ground because of cold winds and lack of moisture.

Does the strange and hairy Abominable Snowman really exist? Many people claim they've seen this two-legged giant wandering in the Himalayan Mountains. But scientists have so far only seen its footprints and say they're three times bigger than a normal person's prints.

33

Winter Log

WOW! THIS IS REALLY FUN!

There are so many things to see and do in winter, sometimes it's hard to remember them all. That's why we're giving you these charts to write and draw on. If you run out of room you can make your own charts in a little notebook. That way you can carry them with you, and maybe even hand them in as a school project.

ONE DAY I ATE 425 WORMS!

WELL.... MY HOUSE WAS COVERED WITH SNOW ONE DAY...

Most Amazing Winter Days

Date	Time	What I Saw

Special Things I've Done

Date	Time	What I Did

Signs of Winter or Spring

Date	Time	What I Saw

Interesting Tracks I've Seen

Date	Who Made Them	What They Looked Like

WOW! WHO MADE THIS.... ME?!?

I SAW YOU, DOES THAT COUNT?

Interesting Birds and Animals I've Seen

Animal or Bird: _____

Date: _____ Time: _____

Notes: _____

_____

_____

Interesting Birds and Animals I've Seen

Animal or Bird: _____

Date: _____ Time: _____

Notes: _____

_____

_____

Interesting Birds and Animals I've Seen

Animal or Bird: _____

Date: _____ Time: _____

Notes: _____

_____

_____

Interesting Birds and Animals I've Seen

Animal or Bird: _____

Date: _____ Time: _____

Notes: _____

_____

_____

Interesting Birds and Animals I've Seen

Animal or Bird: _____

Date: _____ Time: _____

Notes: _____

_____

_____

Interesting Birds and Animals I've Seen

Animal or Bird: _____

Date: _____ Time: _____

Notes: _____

_____

_____

Interesting Birds and Animals I've Seen

Animal or Bird: _____

Date: _____ Time: _____

Notes: _____

_____

_____

Interesting Birds and Animals I've Seen

Animal or Bird: _____

Date: _____ Time: _____

Notes: _____

_____

_____

HOW DO YOU SPELL RIIINOCEROS!?!

EEKS! REMEMBER THAT HUGE CAT I SAW?

WINTER WORD SEARCH

All the words in this puzzle are things you can do or see this winter, as well as things you can read about in this book. We've started it for you by drawing a line around "tracks" and striking it off the list. Do the same with the other words, but be careful because they can run in any direction and can also cross and overlap. When you've circled all the words in the puzzle, the letters that remain will spell out an amazing fact about owls. *A Helpful Hint: starting at the top left hand corner of the puzzle and moving from left to right, jot down the leftover letters in the order they appear.*

YOU NEED A BIRD BRAIN TO DO THIS!?!

GROUNDHOG DAYS
HAPPY
HAT
HOCKEY
HOLIDAY
ICE
INSULATION
INUIT
KEEPING WARM
MIGHTY MITES
MITTEN
NOVEMBER
PLAY

POLAR BEAR
PUCK
RAIN
SCARF
SHIVERING
SKATING
SLIP
SNOWSHOES
TOBOGGAN
~~TRACKS~~
WHIZ
WIND

CROSS COUNTRY SKIING

BEDWARMER
BIRDFEEDER
BOOTS
COLD

CRYSTALS
DR. ZED
FROZEN
GOGGLES

Answer on page 128

```
G O P W L S G O G G L E S S R A I N
N N A I R E A N M R E B M E V O N O
A A I Z L I N H I G B I D T R S D I
G R S I T S O H E R Y E C I A Y N T
G A I S K C E E B E E T T M E A R A
O E C T K S C A R F H V A Y N D P L
B B E E E O Y P D L E I I T N G B U
O R Y O T H T R H E D A N H Y O L S
T A H I G M I T T E N H U G S H T N
P L A Y A B N D R N T H I I E D G I
D O P F R O Z E N W U H T M L N N S
D P P A D R M K H A N O D O T U I L
H N Y E Y R C I S A N L C H E O T A
A R I A A M Z O U K S I E S R R A T
S N O W S H O E S K C D U S S G K S
T L D S T O O B D C E A E I G O S Y
H E T C I T Y B L U O Y R C K S R R
B A M R A W G N I P E E K D W A Y C
```

WINTER: Out of This World

This winter scene was painted by the famous artist [   ]ek Pesek. If you guessed it's part of the icy lowlands of Antarctica or even a snow-covered valley in the Arctic, you'd be wrong.

You'll have to travel farther than the North or S[   ]h Pole to find a scene like this one. In fact, you'll have to leave Earth. Where is this place? To find out, turn the page . . .

Another beautiful purple sunrise, gray snowy patches on red rocks and temperatures of –190°C/ –310°F. Brrr... this is a typical winter's day on Mars. Think you'd like to visit?

If so, be prepared for a winter that lasts up to 12 months. Why is winter so long? It takes the planet Mars 23 months to travel once around the sun, almost twice the time it takes Earth to make the same trip. Not only this, but Mars is about one-and-a-half times farther away from the sun than Earth is. The average temperature there is twice as cold as it ever gets here. You'll warm up a bit if you take a trip to the Martian equator, but temperatures there still don't get much warmer than –22°C/–7.6°F, although sometimes a heat wave will bring what we call a cold winter day.

One other reason it's so cold on Mars is that the air is very thin. Living there would be something like living on top of a mountain that's three times as high as Mount Everest.

You'll never see snow falling on Mars. It'll appear before your eyes. The atmosphere on Mars is made up mainly of a gas called carbon dioxide. When temperatures drop to –80°C/–112°F, carbon dioxide gas near the ground freezes and becomes solid dry ice. This dry ice looks like gray fluff between the red rocks and craters.

Only at the North and South Poles of Mars will you see anything that looks like our snow on Earth. Scientists have discovered thin ice at the Martian poles. This is exciting news. If there's frozen water on Mars, could there be life too? This is something that scientists must still explore.

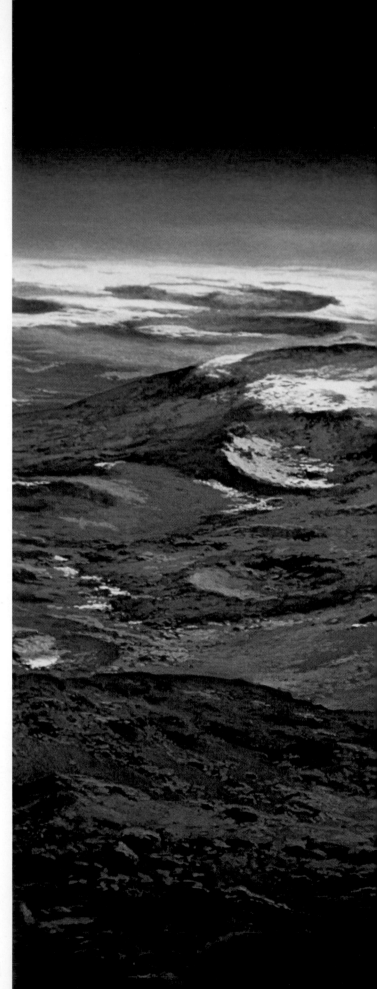

Consultant: Bob MacDonald

THE SNOW BEARS

Three small, black spots slide slowly across the glimmering white snow. What could they be? They move closer and – yes – they're two eyes and a nose belonging to a mother polar bear, almost invisible in the snowy world that surrounds her...

It's July and the polar bear is showing her two cubs how to hunt. Normally her playful cubs can't stay still for even a moment, but their mother has been very strict about how they should behave when she's trying to catch their dinner. So they sit motionless, some distance away, while their mother edges slowly forward, belly to the ground, eyes glued to the breathing hole in the ice where a seal may eventually appear. As the she-bear tenses, the cubs almost stop breathing, afraid to so much as twitch.

Suddenly, two black nostrils break the surface of the water and the cubs hear a seal sucking in air, then ... whoosh! The she-bear turns on the ice, a large seal grasped firmly in her powerful jaws, and her cubs, unable to sit still a moment longer, run towards her. This ringed seal will make a fine feast for the bears, who all need to eat a great deal so they'll be fat and sleek before the hard winter comes again.

Late last October the she-bear had made herself a den. Using her sharp claws to dig out a snowbank and her warm body to firm and smooth the inside walls, she scooped and pressed until she had built a large igloo-like room, linked to the outside by a tunnel. By the time the first snowstorm blocked off the entrance, she was fast asleep, resting for the dark December day when her two babies would be born.

Blizzards were undoubtedly raging outside on the day when, snug inside her den, she gave birth to two guinea pig-sized cubs. To keep her blind, deaf and hairless babies warm, she tucked them between her legs near her rich milk supply. Well-fed and contented, the cubs grew quickly.

By March the time had come for the youngsters to discover the outside world. The she-bear dug a way out and nudged her cubs into the sunlight. All she could think about was food — she hadn't eaten since October. However, her cubs, their stomachs full of milk, just wanted to explore this exciting new world. So while their mother scratched under the snow for plants, the two frisky youngsters tumbled and slid on the glistening snow.

Until her cubs became used to the cold, the she-bear kept them close to the den. But within a few days she was able to lead them to the frozen ice of a sheltered bay where she caught her first real meal of the year, a seal. To keep her growing family supplied with food during the summer, the she-bear will have to lead them further and further north where the ice hasn't melted, because without pack ice it's almost impossible to hunt seals.

Wandering over the ice with their mother, learning different ways of catching seals, will be the way of life for the cubs for the next year. The following summer they too will be hunting and once their mother knows they can survive, usually when they're two and a half, she will leave them. By then it will be time for her to prepare a new den while her older offspring will spend another year or two roaming the ice, growing bigger and stronger, until it is time for them to find mates.

Polar Bears Up Close

A sensible dresser
A polar bear is well built for life in a chilly world – it wears *three* coats. On top is a layer of oily, water- shedding fur, below that, dense underfur and beneath its skin is a thick layer of fat.

Twinkletoes on ice
A polar bear spends most of its life walking on ice, yet it seldom slips. That's because hair grows on the bottom of its paws for non-skid traction (it's useful padding for noiseless hunt- ing, too). Also, its long, sharp claws grip the ice well even when the bear is short-distance sprinting at speeds up to 40 km per hour/25 mph.

Teddy bear ears
And do its ears get cold? Not at all – they're small and furry, a bit like built-in earmuffs.

Summer coolers
Polar bears that live around Hudson Bay don't move north during the summer; instead, they move inland and feed on grasses, berries, bird eggs – just about anything, in fact. On hot summer days, these polar bears keep cool by digging down to the per- mafrost (a layer of earth that is always frozen), then crawling into this refresh- ing "ice box." Ah, bliss!

Super sniffers
Imagine smelling your dinner from many miles away or sniffing out a seal through a thick layer of hard-packed snow. Polar bears do it all the time.

Unsinkable — almost
The layer of fat that helps to keep a polar bear warm acts as a life jacket in water and, along with air bubbles trapped in the underfur, keeps the bear afloat.

Paddle feet
The polar bear's front paws make excellent paddles, and the hind legs can be used as rudders for steering.

Home sweet home
Only a pregnant bear dens up for winter. The temperature inside her snug snow den is 21°C/70°F warmer than the air outside. She sleeps a lot but gets up occasionally to adjust the temperature by poking a hole in the roof or closing it up with snow.

Polar bears' new neighbors
Polar bears are not an endangered species but their lives are in danger as more people move into the north: for example, oil spills and other pollution can harm the seals they depend on for food. Canada is playing a leading role in looking for ways to help the polar bear, as more than half the world's population of these handsome beasts lives in its arctic regions.

Loners
All polar bears other than mothers and babies are loners, wandering summer and winter in search of food, seeking shelter during the most terrible storms. Males and females are together only at mating time, so fathers never see their babies.

Olde Tyme Winter Wis-dumb?

Would you like to know without listening to the radio what weather's coming up? You don't need a crystal ball, a computer or even a weather satellite.

Long ago farmers, hunters, sailors and fishermen—in fact, anyone who was outside a lot—could tell what weather was coming by observing things. Here are some bits of their olde-tyme winter wisdom. Believe them? Oldtimers swear they're all true. You can see if you agree with them by watching for some of these signs. You may be surprised.

Autumn Signs of a Hard Winter to Come

- The new bark on trees is thicker than usual.
- Geese and ducks migrate earlier.
- There are more nuts on trees.
- Beavers build extra-large houses.
- Wild animals have thicker fur.
- Onions have a tougher, thicker skin.

- Woolly caterpillars have wider brown bands on their bodies.

Winter Signs that Fair Weather is on the Way
- Prairie dogs are playful.
- Big snowflakes.
- Dogs rub themselves on things.
- Moles dig in the earth while there's frost on the ground.

- Cats wash their ears a lot.

Winter Signs that Snow and/or Cold Weather is on the Way
- Hares seek shelter in the lowlands.
- Cows face south while grazing.
- Pigs squeal loudly.
- The moon has a halo around it.
- Fires burn fast with a blue flame.
- Willow grouse perch high in trees.

- Cats sit with their tails toward the fire.

45

LONG CLAWS

written and illustrated by James Houston

This story is based on true events that occurred one winter in that vast and lonely Arctic region west of Hudson Bay in Canada's Northwest Territories. Inuit (Eskimo) hunters still talk of the ghost-like owl and the terrifying bear, and of how a brother and sister, Pitohok and Upik, valiantly struggled to bring food to their starving family . . .

Pitohok and Upik had not long been out of the igloo before they came running back inside.

"An owl helped us! Look! We found these fish where she scratched the snow. Four big ones!" Upik clutched the frozen lake trout in her arms, displaying them like precious silver toys.

Upik handed her mother the largest fish, and right away she held it over the small flame of her stone lamp until it softened slightly.

"We must treasure our hunger before a feast," she whispered as she passed the lake trout and her sharp-curved ulu knife around to every member of the family. Then she looked from her two youngest children to Pitohok and Upik, to her old father lying on a fur-covered sleeping platform made of snow. She was wondering how they would all survive the hard winter now that her husband was no longer living. There was no one to hunt for them.

Pitohok, her son, had a smooth, brown face and quick, dark eyes. His teeth were square and strong. He and his sister wore fur parkas, pants and boots all made of caribou skins which made them both look plump. You could only tell their hunger by the dark shadows underneath their wide cheekbones.

When people first looked at Upik, it gave them pleasure, for they could see that she had black, shiny eyes, white teeth and a wide, clear face. When her parka hood was pushed back, they could see the luster of her blue-black hair as it hung in two braids thickened by willow sticks and bound stiff with beads.

"Grandfather," Pitohok said, "the fish has given us enough strength to travel. Tell me where that last caribou is buried so I might go and find it."

"Oh, it is far from here," his grandfather answered. "Too great a distance for you to go alone."

Pitohok looked at his sister and wondered if she might have enough strength to walk with him on such a journey.

"Tell me where it lies?" Pitohok asked again.

"It is three days hard walking west of here," his grandfather said. "Near the Crooked River. Out on that plain last summer a young male caribou fell before my rifle. A strong wind was blowing and it began to snow. A great feeling of weakness came over me. I had no way to carry home that caribou and no time to build a proper cache to hide it. I knew that the heavy snows would drift over its body, hiding all but its horns from sight. So I turned its antlers high so that someone might find it later." He looked at Pitohok. "But it is too great a journey for one person without dogs."

"I will go with him," said Upik.

"Yes, she could help him," said their mother.

Their grandfather closed his eyes. "It is our only chance. If you two make such a journey, you must search for a short hill near the river, climb to its peak and carefully study the land beyond. I believe that you will see that caribou's antlers standing wind-blown, clear of snow. It is bad that we had to break up the sled and burn its wood in the coldest days of winter. And it is sad that the dogs are gone," he said. "But it is good that we are all alive, and I will try hard to think of some way to make a sled for you."

"We will need to dig for that caribou," Pitohok said, "but we cannot find the snow shovel."

"Of course you can't find the shovel," their grandfather said. "I warned all of you that it should have been left lying flat. Someone in this camp stood it upright in the snow. That shovel has a soul like any one of us, like fish, like birds, like caribou, like every other thing. When someone left it standing, it did just what you or I would do. As soon as it grew dark, that shovel ran away. Why not? It doesn't want to stand in the cold, waiting to be a slave to any one of us!"

Pitohok and his sister did not pause long to puzzle over their grandfather's old-fashioned ideas before hunger made them think again of food. They were desperate. No one in their family had eaten anything save that single fish for six long days.

Upik looked into her mother's eyes. She could see hunger there and fear.

"Sleep well now," their mother told them. "Tomorrow when your grandfather looks at the sky it will be decided whether you will go or stay."

"If you cannot find the shovel," their grandfather told Pitohok, "you can take my old snow knife to dig with."

That night the grandfather asked Pitohok's mother to soak two caribou skins in water. When she had done this, he carefully folded each of them lengthwise six times and curved them up on the ends until they started to look like a pair of sled runners. These he placed outside to freeze.

Upik's mother remained awake sewing by her lamp throughout the night so that she could give her two older children each a pair of warm new caribou-skin boots. In the morning the wind was down, but it was bitter cold.

"Bring in the frozen runners," said the grandfather. "If they are hard enough, I shall show you how to build a small sled using only what we have." The old man examined the two frozen skins that he had so carefully shaped into sled runners. They were straight, not much longer than his outstretched arms, and frozen as hard as any wood.

Using an old fashioned bow drill, the grandfather placed one end in his mouth, turned the string of a short bow around its shaft, then made it whirl around as he drew the bow swiftly back and forth,

twisting its sharp nail bit. Quickly he drilled three holes in the tops of each folded caribou-skin runner and forced strong braided caribou sinew through each of these holes.

"Hand me those last three fish," the old man said.

Pitohok passed them to his grandfather.

The grandfather lashed down the stiffly frozen trout on top of the runners so they would serve as crossbars. In this way he was able to bind together a sturdy makeshift sled.

"Hand me those pulling straps," he said to Upik's mother.

He drilled two more holes and attached the straps to the front of the sled. His grandson came and stood before him while he adjusted the long straps to Pitohok's shoulders.

"Now," said their grandfather. "Here is my old rifle and the only two brass cartridges left to us. I have loaded these with the last two pinches of gunpowder we possess. Bullets are usually made with lead, but we have none. I have had to carve two of stone to fit into these cartridge casings. Stone-nosed bullets are strong enough, but I must warn you that they sometimes break and fly apart.

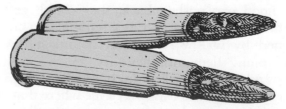

"Go with strength," their grandfather sighed. "If you can find that buried caribou, we may all live to see summer come again."

Upik and Pitohok pulled on their warmest clothing, tied up a roll of caribou sleeping skins.

"I won't come back until I have the meat," Pitohok told his grandfather.

Upik and Pitohok bent and went out the long snow tunnel that protected their igloo from the Arctic winds. Their mother followed them outside. Looking at each other, they could find no words to say between them. Their mother held her youngest daughter Kanajuk's hand as she watched Upik and Pitohok trudge away, dragging the small frozen sled behind them. Tears came into her eyes, for she wondered whether she would ever see her children again.

Beyond the igloo, the vast, flat white snow plain stretched all around them. Far to the east lay Hudson Bay, to the south, frozen Kasba Lake. To the north and west the land continued endlessly toward distant blue snow-covered mountains and oceans that they had never seen.

Upik and Pitohok traveled westward. The late winter sun faded and soon the whole sky was hidden by a heavy blanket of gray clouds that stretched to all the far horizons of the enormous snow-covered land. Only the painful squeal of snow beneath their soft skin boots broke the silence that hung around them.

As it grew dark, fine snowflakes floated down from the western sky. Then gusts of wind came moaning across the land, driving the fine snow upward into whirling, twisting forms that scurried like ghosts across the lonely plain.

Pitohok stopped and quickly drew the snow knife from beneath the lashings of the sled. He licked both sides of the long, thin antler blade until it was glazed with ice and would slice smoothly into the hard snow beneath his feet. Pitohok cut each snow block carefully and stood them around him in a small circle, cleverly piling them until they curved in at the top to form a dome. Upik packed dry snow into the chinks between the blocks. She could feel the force of the cold wind increasing and Upik knew that any weakness in their igloo might allow it to be broken and torn to pieces. Their house of snow was just big enough for the two of them to curl inside. She hoped

it would hold. They would not have a second chance to build an igloo, and without one they could not stay alive.

Upik stuffed their caribou sleeping robes through the low entrance, and Pitohok yelled out to her against the howling wind, "Push the sled inside as well. We may have to eat it before this storm has ended."

He was right. The blizzard raged and screamed over their small shelter for three long, gloomy days and terrifying nights, leaving them weaker than before with fear and hunger. During the storm their igloo trembled like a frightened rabbit. But it held together.

On the fourth morning they heard the wind moaning and dying. Pitohok looked at the three frozen trout that formed their small sled. "Tomorrow we will have to eat one of the fish, or we will not have the strength to travel. Two fish should be enough to hold the sled together."

That night Upik unlashed the lake trout which had been the sled's center crossbar and placed it between herself and the caribou robe beneath her. She slept on top of it all night. In the morning her body heat had thawed the fish enough for them to eat. They shared it with the eagerness of a pair of wild animals.

They traveled all that day and built another igloo and slept again. When they crawled out at dawn, Pitohok pointed into the west. "Do you see something strange over there?"

He cupped his mittened hands together and boosted his sister high. She shaded her sharp eyes and examined the flat horizon.

"It's the hill!" she cried. "And beyond it I can see a long blue streak that looks like ice. It must be the Crooked River."

"Hurry," said Pitohok. "We must find that caribou while the light is strong."

It was almost evening when they reached the snow-clad hill. It was not much taller than two men standing one on the shoulders of the other, but still in this dead, flat land it looked like an enormous mountain. Eagerly Pitohok climbed and just as he neared the top, a snowy owl took flight across the plain.

Upik, when she saw it, excitedly crouched down and secretly sang a song:

"White owl, I sing to you.

Softly I sing to you.

Owl, my helping spirit."

"Look! Look out there where the owl is flying," called Pitohok. "I can see the caribou antlers standing upright. But do you see something moving toward the antlers through the blue shadows of the snowdrifts?"

"Yes, I see it," Upik called up to him. "It's dark brown and humped over like a dog."

"It's kugvik the wolverine!" said Pitohok. "Look at the way that one moves and digs. They're the worst meat robbers in the world. Quick! I need the rifle."

Upik untied their grandfather's rifle from the sled and carried it up to her brother. Pitohok sat down on the snow and, reaching into his small leather bag, took out the two precious brass cartridges and examined their stone noses. Pitohok selected one, opened the rifle and placed the cartridge in its breech.

Pitohok held his grandfather's heavy rifle steady by resting his elbows on his knees. He closed one eye and took careful aim at the dark wolverine that was digging with its sharp claws through the hard-packed snow, trying to get at the caribou.

Upik jumped back when she heard the heavy rifle boom and echo across the wide snow plain.

"I missed," said Pitohok, his voice full of disappointment.

"That's no wonder," Ukik called up to him. "The bullet that you fired broke into three small pieces. I saw the bits of stone fall onto the snow. But the noise of the rifle frightened the wolverine. He's running away!"

Pitohok came leaping down the hill and lashed the rifle onto the sled. "Follow me!" he said, snatching up the long straps. "We must reach that caribou before night comes."

The first stars twinkled in the sky as they came up to the caribou antlers that stood above the snow.

Pitohok stared in wonder at his sister. He whispered, "Is that grandfather's shovel standing in the snow beside the antlers? Are we seeing something magic?"

"Is it truly ours?" said Upik.

"Yes, it's ours," said Pitohok, bending as he stared at this familiar wooden shape and its worn leather stitching. "I'd know that snow shovel anywhere. I've dug with it so many times."

Grandfather must have left it here last autumn," Upik said. "When he was growing weak and it was dark and storming."

Pitohok drew the snow knife from beneath the lashings of the sled and paced out a circle for their igloo.

"I am going to build right on top of the caribou, leaving only its horns outside," Pitohok said, "so that wolverine won't come back here in the night and steal the meat from us."

When their new igloo was completed, Upik looked up and saw the cold-faced winter moon rising in the eastern sky. She crawled into the igloo, and Pitohok sighed and said, "Perhaps we don't have to eat. My belly feels full just knowing that we're going to sleep on top of all this rich caribou meat." He patted their snow floor. "Imagine how glad our family will be when we return with such a treasure."

They rose early in the morning and tried again to forget their hunger as they broke the igloo's side walls. Using the snow knife and the shovel, they dug up the frozen caribou and lashed it onto the small sled.

Before they left, Pitohok carefully stood the shovel upright in the snow. He smiled and said, "If you can walk, please hurry home to our grandfather and tell him we are coming."

The snow shovel did not move or seem to hear his words.

Pitohok took up the carrying straps and together they headed back toward their home. They hauled the welcome weight of meat behind them, following their own footprints eastward, hurrying until it was almost dark. Then they built a small igloo and slept, exhausted.

Many times the following morning Upik looked back at the precious caribou lashed to the creaking sled. She tried to fight off her hunger by saying, "Just think of the wonderful smell that meat will make as it simmers in our mother's pot."

The morning sun had risen high above the plain when Pitohok stopped and pushed up his wooden goggles. He shaded his eyes, then pointed at a small, dark speck far away. "Do you see it?"

"Yes, what is it?" Upik asked him as she watched it moving very slowly toward them across the endless plain of snow.

"I don't know what it is," said Pitohok as he pulled down his goggles to protect his eyes again. "It's not a caribou or a man. But it is certainly something that's alive."

"Let us hurry home," said Upik. "I don't like the look of that moving spot. It sways from side to side in a heavy way that frightens me."

By midafternoon the brown speck had grown much larger.

"It is moving faster than we can walk. What is it?" Upik asked her brother.

"I am not sure," he said, handing her one of the straps. "Let us run for a little while together, then walk, and run again. Perhaps it will turn and go away."

In the late afternoon they had to stop and rest because their legs were too tired to go on.

"Can you tell me now what it is?" Upik gasped. "That thing that is coming closer to us?"

"Yes," Pitohok said. "It is Akla, a barren ground grizzly bear. It is moving in our footprints, following our scent."

"I am afraid," said Upik. "I have never seen an akla, but I have heard terrible things about them. That is why the hunters call them Long Claws."

"Let us walk fast again," said Pitohok.

When the sun started to sink into the west, Pitohok knew that they could not get away from the huge, hump-shouldered grizzly that came shambling after them, rolling its enormous hips, gaining on them with every step it took.

"We've got to do something," Pitohok gasped, and now his voice was full of fear. "That akla's going to catch us no matter how fast we walk. And if we run now, it may get excited and attack. Grizzlies are tireless in following their prey and can make short fast bursts of speed. Grandfather told me that strong aklas in their prime can sometimes catch a running caribou."

"What shall we do?" his sister asked him, and Pitohok could tell by her voice that she was almost crying.

Pitohok stopped and drew his grandfather's rifle out from under the sled lashings and put their last stone-nosed cartridge inside its barrel. He saw the way his sister looked at him and said, "I hope we won't have to use it."

He stood the rifle upright in the snow. Then quickly he bent and unlashed the frozen caribou and rolled it off the sled. With his short, sharp knife he cut the bindings that held the sled together. As it fell

52

apart, Pitohok grabbed one of the runners. Whirling it around his head, he flung it as far as he could along the trail toward the oncoming grizzly.

The akla stopped and raised its massive head and stared at the two human creatures. Pitohok and Upik could hear the akla's stomach rumbling with hunger as he ambled forward and sniffed the folded caribou skin. Placing one paw upon it, the grizzly tore it into pieces with its teeth and began devouring it.

Pitohok knelt down beside the frozen caribou and grasped it by its front and rear legs. "Quick!" he said to Upik. "Help me heave this meat onto my shoulders."

She did so, scarcely able to believe how heavy it was.

As soon as Pitohok rose to his feet, he started walking, hurrying once more along their own trail that would lead them home.

"You bring the rifle and the snow knife and the last two fish," he called back to his sister. "One sleeping robe will have to do us. Tie it around yourself. Leave the other one. Move!" he said, and Upik could hear a note of horror creeping into his voice again. "Don't let that Long Claws near you!"

Upik's legs ached with tiredness, but she hurried after him, afraid to look back, afraid she would find the grizzly close behind her.

The evening sun turned red as it slid down and touched the long, flat, white horizon. Pitohok looked back, then groaned beneath the heavy weight of caribou. "Long Claws is coming after us again," he warned her. "Give him a fish. Hurry and fling it back toward him."

Upik did as she was told.

Pitohok looked again, then slowed his pace. "He's lying down," Pitohok gasped. "He's eaten the trout. He looks now as if he's going to sleep." It was growing dark and Pitohok was staggering with tiredness. "Hold onto me," he groaned. "Help me. I've got to make my feet carry me over that next snow ridge so the akla won't see us stop to build our igloo."

When they were beyond the huge bear's sight, Pitohok collapsed, letting the caribou fall to the snow. Upik helped him up, but Pitohok was so exhausted that he could scarcely rise. With the snow knife Upik cut a shallow grave-like hole and they slid the caribou in and carefully covered it with snow. They built their igloo on top of it.

Once inside, Pitohok wedged a snow block firmly into place, trying to jam the entrance. "Let us share our one last fish," he said. "I have never been so hungry or so tired in all my life."

Even as they gnawed on the frozen trout, they listened carefully. But they could not hear the akla. Upik did not finish her share of the fish, so exhausted was she from their terrible journey. They rolled themselves in the caribou robe and slept, not knowing if the akla would let them live to see the next day dawn again.

When Pitohok awoke, he said, "The weather's changed. Can you not smell and feel spring's dampness in the air?"

Cautiously he cut away the entrance block and crawled outside. Upik followed him. The land was blanketed in lead-gray fog of a kind that hangs heavily above the snow, hiding everything from view. The huge akla might have been very close to them or very far away.

Pitohok dug up the caribou and, cutting a larger entrance in their igloo, shoved the frozen animal outside.

"There is Long Claws. He is waiting for us," Upik whispered with terror in her voice.

Pitohok looked up and saw the dark outline of the akla standing watching them. It was less than a stone's throw away, its wide back glistening with silver hoarfrost that made the coarse hair on its massive shoulders bristle like countless sharp steel needles.

"Shall I try to shoot him now?" Pitohok whispered to his sister.

"No," she said. "No! I'm afraid that last bullet will break and the noise will only anger him."

"Then hurry," he cried. "Help me get this caribou up onto my back. I don't know how far I can carry it today. My legs feel weak as water. But we've got to get it home."

Swaying its huge head back and forth, the grizzly let a low growl rumble from its throat. He was so close now that for the first time Upik could see the akla's long, sharp claws. They cut deep furrows in the snow when it came shambling toward them. Its beady black eyes watched every move they made.

"Leave our caribou sleeping skin in front of the igloo. That may fool him," Pitohok whispered. "If he goes inside, he will surely smell the place where the caribou lay last night. He may stay there digging long enough for us to lose him."

Together they hurried away, trying to hide themselves from Long Claws in the heavy ice fog. They walked and walked until they came to a river bed that seemed familiar to them. Violent winds had blown one bank free of snow, but in the swirling fog they could not tell where it would lead them. Pitohok struggled up onto the stones that formed the bank of the frozen river. His sister had to help him by pushing at his back.

"Be careful not to leave a single track up here," Pitohok gasped. "Step from rock to rock," he warned her. "The wind is at our back. If the akla cannot see us or smell our footprints, we may lose him."

Together they traveled on the stony river bank until about midday, following a twisted course, leaving no path behind them.

"I hope we are far enough away from him," Pitohok gasped. "I can walk no farther."

He sank to his knees and let the heavy weight of the caribou sag down until it rested on the stones. He lay against it, his chest heaving as he tried to catch his breath. Although the air was stinging cold, Upik had to kneel and wipe the sweat from her brother's face.

"He's gone," Upik sighed, glad to rest the heavy rifle in the snow. She looked around herself in the thickening fog. "Which way do we go now?"

Pitohok peered over his shoulder and felt cold sweat trickling down his spine. He could see no sign of the sun. Everything was hidden by a wall of fog.

"I . . . I don't know," he admitted. "I was trying so hard to get away from the akla that now . . . we're lost!"

Pitohok struggled painfully onto his knees and looked in all directions. He saw nothing but gray ice fog that drifted in phantom swirls along the frozen river.

"Oh, I wish someone would help us," Upik whispered aloud, and, as if in answer to her words, low toward her out of the fog winged the snowy owl. It stared at her with its huge golden-yellow eyes, then suddenly changed its wing beat, hovering as if by magic at the very edge of the smokelike mists. It seemed to signal Upik, then, turning sharply to the right, the owl flew off, cutting a dark trail through the wall of fog.

Upik stood up. Then, bending, using all her strength, she helped her brother heave the caribou onto his back. She struggled to ease the heavy burden as he painfully stood upright. "We should follow her," said Upik.

Her brother's answer was a moan as he felt the full weight of the frozen caribou settle on his tired, cramped shoulders. "Yes, follow the owl," Pitohok whispered in a voice grown weak from strain.

Upik had to hold her brother to try and keep him from staggering as they walked. She looked back only once at the pitiful zigzag trail that they now left in the snow as Pitohok's strength ran out of him. Both of them had lost all sense of distance and of time. Upik tried desperately to follow the owl's course through the thickening fog, wondering if they would ever reach their home.

They had not gone far before Upik heard a heavy breathing sound. She turned, then screamed in terror when she saw the huge grizzly, its heavy head rolling, its tongue lolling out as it came padding after gasped Pitohok. "I can't do it. My arms are too tired. My whole body is trembling from carrying all this weight. Let him get close to you," he said, "then shoot him . . . in the head!"

Upik stopped and raised the heavy rifle and tried to sight along its wavering barrel. "I can't," she said. "I am afraid . . . afraid this last stone bullet will break." She was weeping.

"Drop the caribou," Upik begged her brother. "Let him take it. We can walk away from him alive. He will stop and eat. Please drop it," Upik whispered to her brother. "I am afraid that akla is going to try to kill you for that meat."

Pitohok hunched his shoulders and struggled forward as though he had not heard her warning. But now Upik could see that he held his short knife in his hand and that he would not give up their prize of meat without a fight.

Once more she heard an angry rumble in the grizzly's throat and saw it reach out with one terrible paw and rake the caribou along the whole length of its back. As its claws hooked against the caribou's

them. It now moved not more than a single pace behind her brother. Upik saw Long Claws raise his head and sniff at the rich burden of caribou which had softened a little because of the heat of Pitohok's body. The grizzly stretched out its neck and licked the frosted nostrils of the caribou.

"What's the matter?" Pitohok asked her. Then turning, he, too, saw the bear. His voice caught in his throat. "You've got to . . . to try and shoot him," antlers, Upik's brother was thrown off balance and stumbled sideways, falling onto both his knees. The big bear moved closer to him. Driven by fear and desperation, Pitohok rose and continued walking, his eyes narrowed, his whole face pale with strain.

The huge akla, with lips drawn back to show its enormous teeth, came after him again. Upik once more raised her grandfather's rifle and looked along its sights. The bear must have heard the safety catch click off, for it stopped and moved back a little.

At that moment, Pitohok whispered hoarsely, "I see the owl again! She's sitting over there, and I think she's on our family's empty food cache. Can it be?" he sobbed. "Are we... almost home?"

Before Upik could answer, the bear moved forward again, and raising up on its hind feet, it struck out angrily at the caribou's plump haunches. Pitohok reeled from the heavy blow and staggered to his knees. Upik saw her brother try to get up, then sink back on the snow.

"I'm finished," he said, "I can't go on."

Upik could see that he had lost his knife. There were tears in Pitohok's eyes, but his teeth were clenched in anger. Pitohok tightened his grip upon the caribou.

"Let go," she pleaded with her brother. "Let him have the meat."

"No," Pitohok said. "If I lose this caribou to that bear and return home with nothing, none of us will live, and I, myself, would die of shame."

He turned away from the hot breath of the snarling grizzly whose great swaying head was not more than an arm's length from his face.

"Run!" Pitohok whispered to his sister. "Run for the igloo and save yourself."

Upik bent and grabbed her brother underneath the arms. "I am not going anywhere without you," she said as she thrust her body around so that she stood directly between her brother and the akla's gaping jaws.

"Don't do that," Pitohok gasped. He was hunched over on the snow like an old man. "Run! Run!" he moaned. "Put the rifle under the caribou to help me support this weight, or I... shall never rise. Run!"

56

Pitohok wept aloud as he whispered, "I can't stand any more." He groaned, "All my strength has gone. It's going black... I'm going to faint."

"You are coming with me, now!" said Upik. "I can see our igloo. It's not far from us. Can you not see it through the fog?"

Upik put her right shoulder underneath the caribou and her left arm around her brother's waist and strained with all her might. Together they rose from the snow and staggered off toward their family's house. Pitohok stumbled again and fell onto one knee. He hung there gasping for breath.

The akla could not help but hear him. It snarled as it took the caribou's hind leg and Pitohok's mitted hand between its crushing jaws.

"*Unalook! Kukikotak!*" Upik screamed at the bear. "We shared our fish with you. Don't you dare to harm my brother. He must take this food home to our family... they are starving... don't you understand?"

The huge bear let go of Pitohok's hand and the caribou's leg and stood there staring at her.

"Quick! Get back on your feet," Upik whispered. "We have only a little way to go."

The grizzly must have seen the snowhouse, too, for suddenly it shambled around in front of them, blocking Pitohok's way.

"I warned you not to hurt my brother," Upik screamed again.

As if ruled by magic, the huge bear stepped back and let them pass.

"Mother! Mother! Come and help us!" Upik waited.

Long Claws turned his head and stared at her when Upik's mother burst out of their igloo entrance. She saw the great humped shoulders of the akla and, like her daughter, screamed at it, then turned and rushed inside again.

Upik tried to take half of the caribou's weight on her own shoulders as she pulled Pitohok to his feet. Slowly he rose, but Upik could see that his knees would not support him.

"Don't drop it now," she said in a stern voice. "We're almost there."

Together they staggered painfully toward the igloo.

"Everything is whirling around," cried Pitohok. "It's going black again...I'm falling...."

Because she no longer had the strength to hold him, Upik and her brother collapsed onto the snow. She shook him, but Pitohok seemed to have lost his power to hear or move or speak. She tried to drag him away toward the igloo, but his arms remained locked tight around their precious burden of meat.

Long Claws turned and came after them, this time snarling like a huge and angry dog. It grasped the caribou's neck in its powerful jaws and started backing away, dragging the carcass and Pitohok, pulling both of them into the invisible wall of fog.

The snow knife, the rifle, and even Pitohok's short knife were gone. Upik had no weapons but her hands and teeth. Crying out for help again, she turned and saw her grandfather come crawling out of the igloo on his hands and knees. He held his huge curved bow in his left mitt and in his mouth he clutched a pair of arrows. Right behind him came their mother, her parka hood blown full of icy wind, screaming, raging to protect her children, ready to do battle with the enormous bear. With her hands outstretched like claws, their mother snatched up the old snow shovel and raced forward to attack.

Upik heard her grandfather call out, "Stop, woman. Hold! If you help me, we can pierce him right from here."

Upik saw her grandfather kneel unsteadily and notch an arrow to the braided string. His hands trembled as he tried with all his might but could not draw the powerful old-fashioned bow. In desperation Upik's mother knelt beside her father, helping him to draw the powerful weapon almost to full curve. The grandfather's muscles quivered as he tried to aim. Upik saw the point of the arrow wavering wildly.

"Don't!" she cried, spreading her arms and running between her grandfather's unsteady arrow and the bear. "You might hit Pitohok."

Looking back, she saw her brother being dragged across the snow behind the bear.

Upik whirled around and ran straight towards the akla, screaming, *"You let go of him! Let go!"*

Surprised, the huge grizzly released the caribou and raised its head.

"Here, this is for you," she said, and reaching into her parka hood, she snatched out the last frozen piece of trout and flung it far beyond the bear.

The akla looked at her, then grunted and turned, moving away from her brother, who still clasped the caribou as fiercely as an Arctic crab. The grizzly snatched up in his mouth the piece of fish that she had saved for him. Then, with his rear hips and frosted shoulders rolling, he disappeared into the silver wall of icy fog.

Pitohok's mother and his grandfather hurried out and knelt beside him, trying to unlock Pitohok's determined grip around the caribou.

Pitohok opened his eyes and stared at them. "I thought that akla would surely snatch the caribou away," he gasped.

"I, too, believed that he would take it from you," his grandfather agreed. "But no human knows exactly what the animals will do."

"Upik was afraid of the akla, and yet she ran and put her body between me and the grizzly's jaws. Grandfather, did you believe my sister would do that?"

"No. I didn't know what she would do. Nobody knows the strength or courage that humans possess until real danger comes to test them."

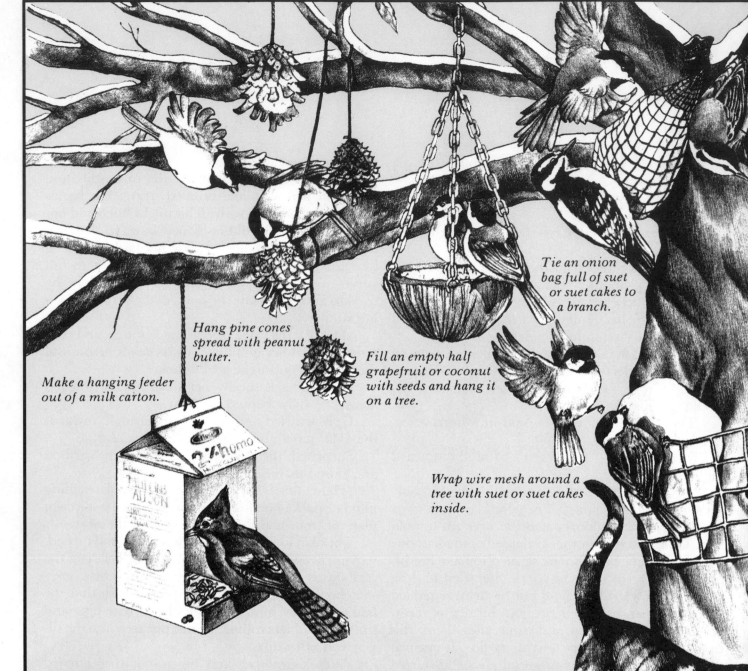

Hang pine cones spread with peanut butter.

Make a hanging feeder out of a milk carton.

Fill an empty half grapefruit or coconut with seeds and hang it on a tree.

Tie an onion bag full of suet or suet cakes to a branch.

Wrap wire mesh around a tree with suet or suet cakes inside.

Eight Simple Bird Feeders for You to Make

Feeding birds is easy and fun. Here are some simple ways to give birds the fat and the seeds they need when it is hard for them to find food.

When to feed birds
In the autumn, birds leave their summer nesting grounds to find new places to spend the winter. By stocking your feeder now, you'll encourage birds to come to your garden all winter. Don't worry about keeping birds from migrating if you feed them. They might stay a few extra days to stock up on food but they will instinctively head south at the right time.

Two things to remember:
1. Birds might take some time before they find your feeder. Help them find it by tying a red ribbon to it.
2. **You must keep feeding the birds once you start. Winter birds will depend on the food and might starve if you leave your feeder empty.**

What to feed birds
Feed them chunks of suet, which you can get from a butcher. Or you can mix peanut butter with equal parts of cornmeal. Wild birdseed, sunflower seeds, peanuts or scraps of meat or fat from the table are good. Fruit, either dried or fresh, is also very welcome.

Tie a chunk of
suet in a tree notch.

Nail an apple crate to a tree
trunk.

Make a hole in a coconut
and hang it from a branch.

A special recipe: suet cakes strictly for the birds
Cut up or mince your suet chunks so that they melt easily. Put the minced suet into a pot over low heat. Stir until it becomes liquid. It is best to heat and cool the suet two or three times. The last time that you melt the suet, mix in wild birdseed and pour into cups or bowls to harden. Remove the suet cake by dipping each cup in hot water after the mixture is hard.

Some hints:
Keep your feeder high enough so cats can't reach the birds.

If possible, hang your feeder near an evergreen tree so that the birds can go into the tree when there is danger.

Be sure to put your feeder where you will be able to reach it when the snow is deep.

Hang your feeder so you can see it easily from a window.

Tree Cheers!

This is a forest of different trees and shrubs that is also a maze. Can you find your way through? You start on the trunk of the Black Spruce and finish when you get to the Juniper. The route runs along branches and trunks and touches each tree or shrub only once. After you have done the maze why not take your book outside and see how many of these trees you can find?

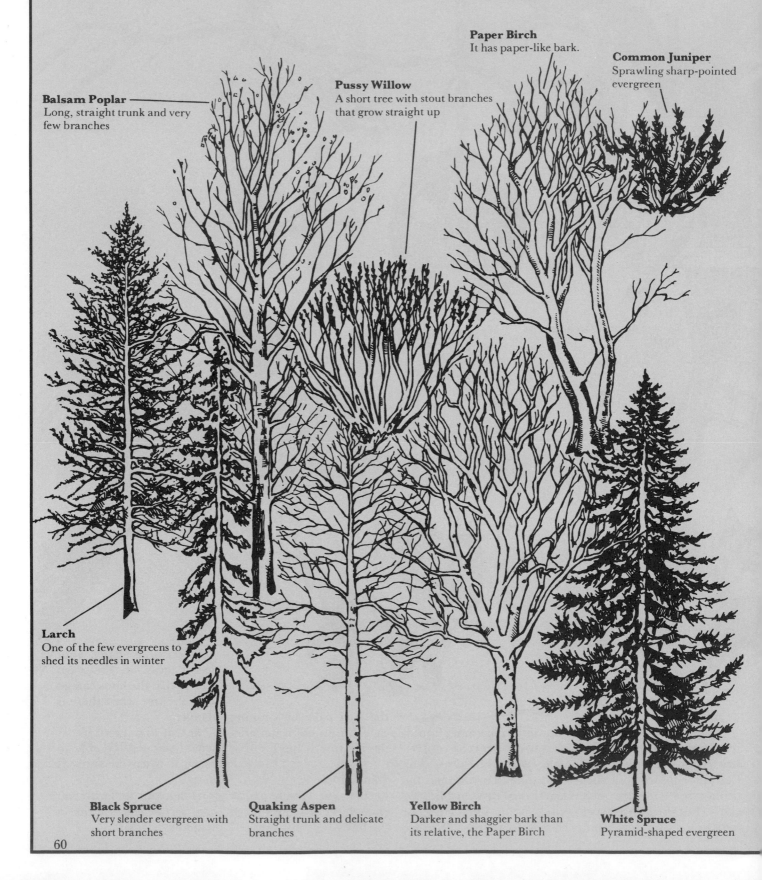

Paper Birch
It has paper-like bark.

Common Juniper
Sprawling sharp-pointed evergreen

Balsam Poplar
Long, straight trunk and very few branches

Pussy Willow
A short tree with stout branches that grow straight up

Larch
One of the few evergreens to shed its needles in winter

Black Spruce
Very slender evergreen with short branches

Quaking Aspen
Straight trunk and delicate branches

Yellow Birch
Darker and shaggier bark than its relative, the Paper Birch

White Spruce
Pyramid-shaped evergreen

60

ANIMALS IN WINTER

These Japanese macaques aren't as silly as they look. To keep warm they soak themselves for hours on end in the mountain hot springs where they live. All animals who live in wintry climates have adapted amazingly well, as you'll see on the pages that follow . . .

If you were a moose, would you walk around in freezing waters? You might, indeed. In winter, grasses are sometimes eas- ier to find at the water's edge than on land and sometimes it's easier to walk in the water than to wade through snow.

The snowshoe hare has to move quickly even in snow to escape from its enemies. Its big, flat feet help it from sinking, while its furry soles keep it from skidding as it races over the ice.

When you live high on a cliff with not much shelter from the blasting winds, a warm coat is very important. That's why the mountain goat's outer guard hairs and woolly undercoat grow longer and longer as winter approaches. As you can see, so do its shaggy leggings and beard.

This red fox has lots of crafty ways for surviving in winter. Right now it's keeping warm in a snow bed that it has dug for itself.

Birds like these whooper swans have a great way of keeping warm when the weather is chilly. They fluff up their feathers so the air that gets trapped in them is warmed by the heat from their bodies. It's just as if they carry their own ski jacket.

The waters in Antarctica are very cold. But that doesn't bother these adélie penguins. They've got a thick layer of fat and a suit of feathers so tightly overlapped they're waterproof.

If you saw this ptarmigan in summer, you probably wouldn't know it. It would be brown to blend in with the grasses. In the fall it is half brown and half white and almost ready for winter.

Why is a snowy owl snowy? It's good camouflage, of course, but white is also an excellent color for northern birds and animals as it helps to keep the heat in their bodies. That's because white hair cells are filled with air—not color.

What's this? Is that a beak you see there, and where are the eyes? That's just what the Antarctic fulmar hopes you'll be: confused. It's hiding from enemies and you can bet it's warmer than it looks under all that snow.

Snowshoe Hare Maze

The life of the snowshoe hare is a very dangerous one because it has to be careful to avoid all the predators you see below and many more besides.

Try to get the hare safely to its home at the bottom right corner of this picture—and watch out for those sharp teeth and claws!

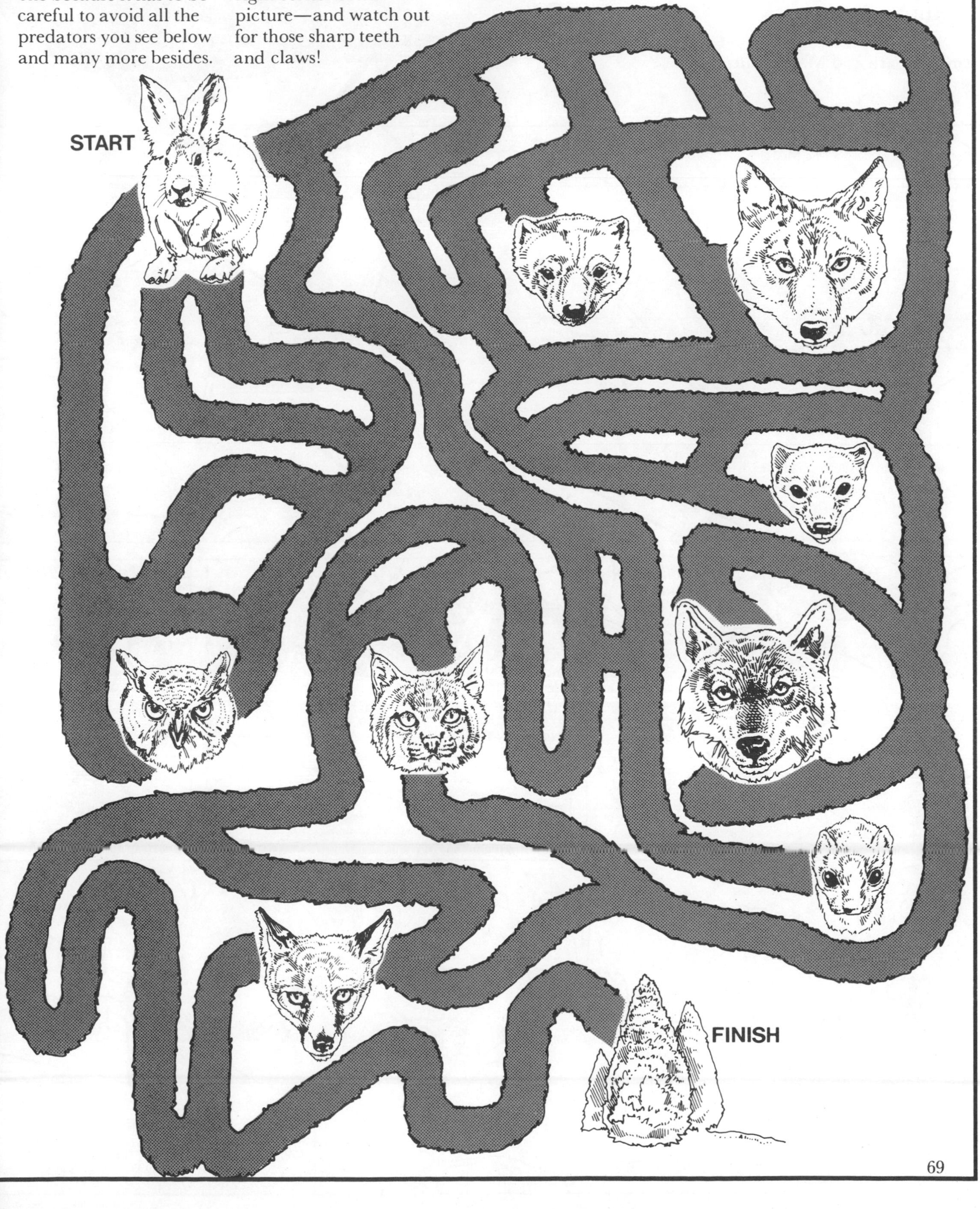

START

FINISH

Nick, Sophia and Mark Mite have invented a shrink drink that makes them small and a grow drink that makes them big again. They are skiing one day and become involved in an amazing animal adventure . . .

by Emily Hearn and Mark Thurman

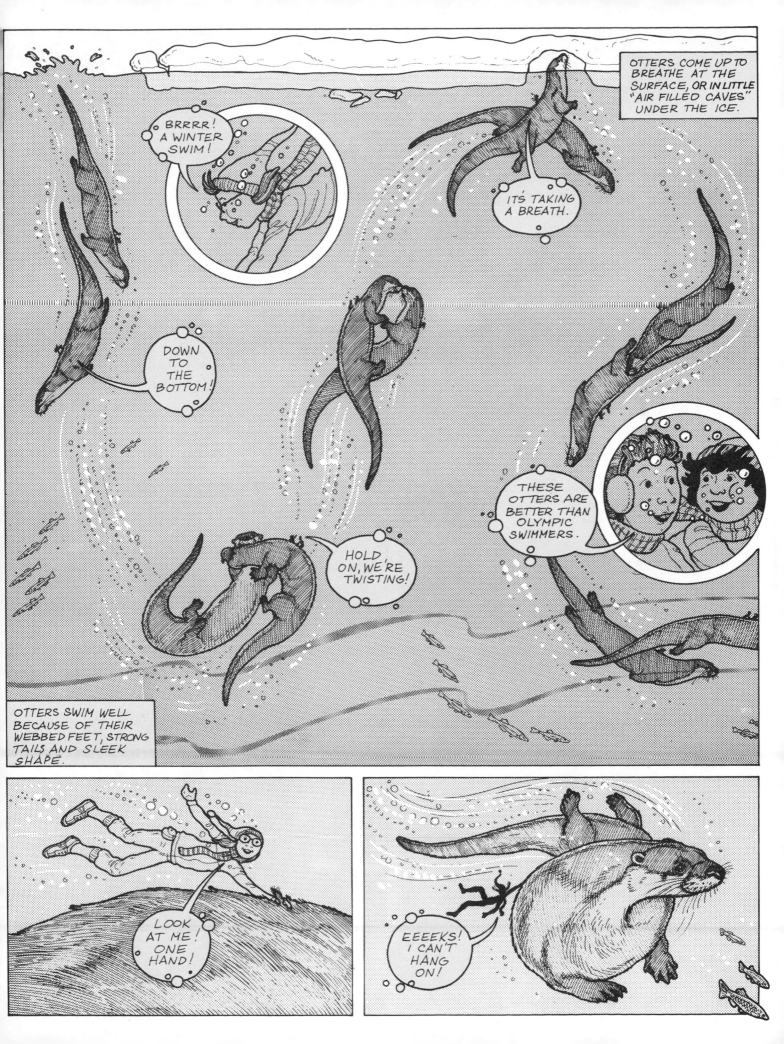

Be a Tracking Detective

RABBIT

RABBIT RUNNING

FOX

RACCOON

If you looked out the window one winter morning upon this woodland scene would you be able to discover what happened during the night by reading the tracks? You can sharpen your tracking skills by looking at this picture and deciding if the clues are true or false.

1. A raccoon walked from the woodpile onto the roof.
True ___ False___
2. A person has recently gone into the cabin.
True ___ False ___
3. The pail was knocked over by a raccoon.
True ___ False ___
4. A mouse was caught by an owl.
True ___ False ___
5. Two deer walked past the cabin.
True ___ False ___
6. The owl swooped on its prey from a tree.
True ___ False ___
7. A mouse visited the water pump.
True ___ False ___
8. The fox was in a hurry.
True ___ False ___
9. The bear stayed in the woods.
True ___ False ___
10. The rabbit hopped past the pump, then ran towards the cabin.
True ___ False ___

How do you rate as a tracker?
8-10 answers correct: Fantastic
5-8 answers correct: Good
Less than 5 answers correct: Better luck next time.

Answers on page 128.

OWL

OWL
SWOOPING DOWN

WING PRINTS

MOUSE

DEER

BEAR

THE LONG COLD SLEEP

When winter comes, animals in cold countries must find a way of getting through the months when food is hard to find. Some animals, like deer, stay active, eating any food they can find. Others migrate to warmer places. Still others simply hide away in a sheltered place and remain there until spring comes round again. They hibernate to survive.

So exactly what is hibernation? It's a sluggish state in which some animals spend the winter. When many animals hibernate, their heart rates, breathing and growth slow down, almost stop, and some may even appear to be dead.

Different animals hibernate in different ways, as you can see in this imaginary scene here . . .

1. Buried toads

Cold-blooded toads must find a place to hibernate where they will not freeze. To do this they sink themselves into some mud. Then they close their nostrils, eyes and mouths and take in small amounts of oxygen through their skin.

2. Snakes in pits

In early fall, snakes eat huge amounts of food to store up fat for winter. Then they head for deep pits where they are protected from surface frosts. Sometimes many thousands of snakes share the same pit.

3. Napping Raccoons

Raccoons sleep only during very cold spells. They often have dens in hollow trees and line them with leaves or wood chips. During mild weather they leave these dens, and you might be able to find their footprints in the snow. If you live in the city, however, you will find raccoons out and about all winter long. City raccoons have a good food supply so do not need to hibernate like their country cousins.

4. Cosy Skunks

Skunks often hibernate in the abandoned dens of groundhogs or foxes, but they will sometimes dig a simple den like this one. A group of skunks will settle down in one den for the winter. It must be crowded, as they are fat indeed!

5. Drowsy Bears

At the first snowfall of winter, the black bear heads for its winter sleeping spot. It sleeps in a cave or on a comfortable bed of boughs under the low branches of an evergreen tree, or even in a hollow log. Many people call this kind of sleep hibernation, but they're wrong. The bear stays warm and relaxed and its heartbeat remains almost normal, whereas in real hibernation the body becomes cold and rigid and the heartbeat slows down. Because bears do not sleep as deeply as true hibernators, they can easily be woken up. So don't shout if you spot what might be a bear's den, you might wake the baby. Female bears—even though they are drowsy—give birth to cubs in January and February.

6. Hanging Bats

Little brown bats hibernate by the hundreds in cool caves where the humidity is very high. Here they hang by their back feet from the ceiling and become covered with sparkling dewdrops of condensation. If the temperature of the cave remains stable they can sleep the winter away, but if the temperature changes they wake.

Groundhog Daze

Rumor has it that on February 2nd groundhogs come out of their burrows, and if they can see their shadows they go back to sleep for another six weeks. No one is quite certain where this superstition came from, but scientists have found that there is no truth to it at all. Nevertheless, groundhogs do have some interesting habits which you can find out more about in this story.

2. By the end of summer they are enormously fat.

1. In summer groundhogs love to sun themselves on warm rocks or along the low branches of trees. The rest of the time they stuff themselves with food.

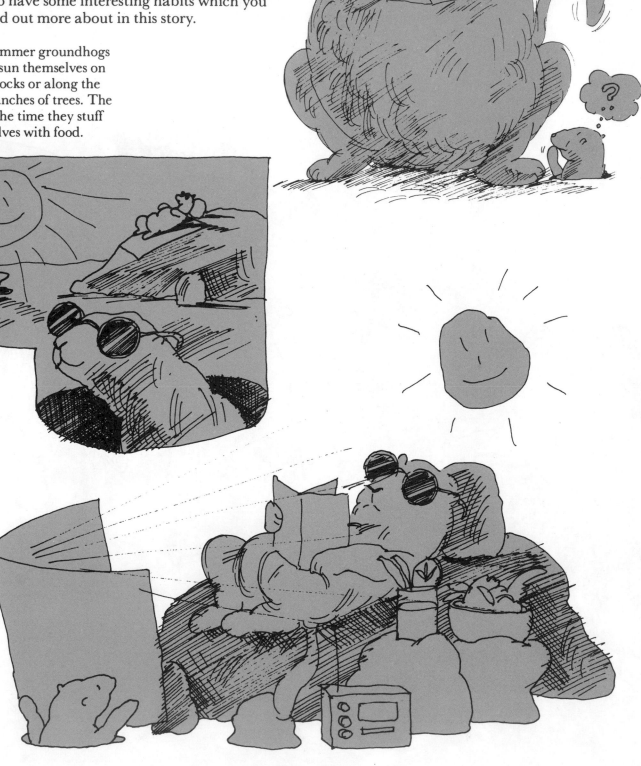

3. Around September they leave their summer burrows, which are often in the middle of meadows, and prepare their denning burrows for winter hibernation in nearby protected places. A feature of the denning burrows is a cozy nesting chamber lined with dry grass and leaves. The groundhogs use this "room" for sleeping, hibernating and nursing their young.

THIS WAY TO DENNING BURROW

8. Groundhogs mate shortly after they come out of their burrows and babies are born a month later.

LOVE YOU ZELDA

4. By October all groundhogs have sealed themselves in their winter dens by plugging the entrance to the nesting chamber with earth and vegetation. The long sleep begins.

6. Groundhogs will wake up every ten days or so and poke their noses outdoors. When snow covers the ground they have to burrow up through it to reach daylight. On mild winter days you can even see them scurrying about on sunny slopes.

7. A groundhog is thin in spring because it has used up its supply of stored fat. The average groundhog loses 30% of its total body weight, and it's very, very hungry.

GROUNDHOG WEIGHT SCALE
GETTING CLOSER
NORMAL
SKINNY
VERY SKINNY
GROWL

9. Groundhogs like to eat fresh green vegetation but it's scarce in the early spring so they occasionally eat snails or insects, or survive on the bark and twigs of cherry trees, sumac and dogwood.

5. During the cold periods of its five to seven month hibernation a groundhog's temperature drops down to only 4°C/39°F and its heartbeat drops from a normal rate of 80 beats per minute to only four or five. Breathing rate and oxygen consumption are greatly reduced.

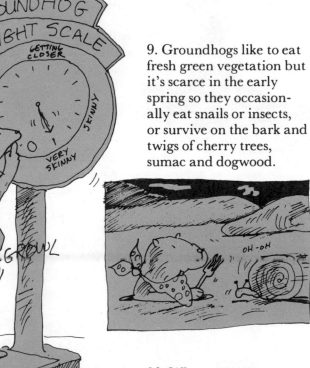

OH-OH

10. When summer arrives, groundhogs move house again back to the meadow. You can often see them peeping out of their special "spy holes" or basking in the warmth.

A Magic Ice Cream Cake

There's a delicious dessert, known as Baked Alaska, that brings a little bit of winter right to the dining room table. It's made from a cake, meringue and ice cream. It's like magic, because even though you put it in a hot oven to cook, the ice cream doesn't melt.

You will need:
a white, sponge or pound cake
a freezer tray of ice cream
4 egg whites at room temperature
8 tablespoons sugar
hand or electric beater
a baking sheet
a large bowl

Ask a grownup to preheat the oven to 500°F.

Getting the ice cream ready
Put any kind of ice cream you like in a freezer tray and squash it down.

To make the meringue
1. Separate the whites from the yolks of the 4 eggs. Do this by cracking the eggs and carefully pouring the yolks from one half of the shell to the other and letting the whites dribble into a bowl. (You might want to ask a grown up to help.)

2. Beat the egg whites until they begin to look like whipped cream. They're perfect when they start to make what looks like mountain peaks when you lift them with the beater. (Stop beating before you do this test or egg white will fly all over the kitchen.) Add the sugar, two tablespoons at a time, beating well after each addition. After about five minutes the mixture will become very stiff and shiny.

"WHY DOESN'T THE ICE CREAM INSIDE THE MAGIC CAKE MELT WHEN IT'S PUT INTO THE HOT OVEN?"

To make the magic cake
1. Place the cake on the baking sheet and cut it in the same shape as your freezer tray.

2. Put some hot water into the sink and dip the bottom of the ice cream freezer tray into the water. (This will loosen the ice cream.)

3. Slide the ice cream out of the tray so it is on top of the cake.

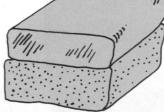

4. Spread the meringue you made earlier over the ice cream and cake so they are completely covered up by about 2.5 cm/1 inch of the meringue.

5. Put the cake into a 500° F oven for 3 to 5 minutes until the meringue is lightly browned. Serve immediately.

Good news! You can make your magic cake up to one hour before dinner. Store it in the freezer until you're about ready for dessert. Then pop it in the oven. The meringue will be lovely and hot and the ice cream will still be frozen.

NOW, HOW'S THIS?

THE REASON IS THAT THE MERINGUE ON THE OUTSIDE OF THE CAKE IS FULL OF AIR BUBBLES. THEY DON'T CONDUCT (OR CARRY) HEAT VERY WELL, SO THEY STOP THE HEAT FROM GETTING TO THE ICE CREAM.

THIS WORKS IN THE SAME WAY THAT THE LAYER OF AIR BETWEEN THE WALLS OF A 'THERMOS' KEEPS THE COLD LIQUID INSIDE FROM BEING WARMED ON A HOT DAY.

by Marilyn Linton

Put on Your Hat to Warm Your Feet
and other great tips for enjoying winter

If your feet are cold you should put on your hat. Sound silly? It's not. This is just one of the very simple tricks to keeping warm in winter. Try it and the other bits of winter outdoors advice in this article.

Warm head, warmer feet

Because your body works hard to pump lots of warm blood to your brain when you become cold, less blood circulates to your feet. By wearing a hat you will keep your head, and your brain, warm so your body will send blood to less important places, such as your feet. Makes sense!

Metal is cold!!!

So never touch anything metal, such as skate blades or ski poles, with your bare hands. You'll find they will stick to it. If this does happen by mistake, warm your skin and the metal with mittens, a jacket or a blanket, and this will get you unstuck.

Loose boots

Your feet stay much warmer if your boots are loose. This allows blood to circulate to them more easily and because layering is a good idea, two pairs of socks are better than one.

Natural eyeglasses

One of the best ways to protect your eyes from snow glare is to make yourself some snow goggles, as the Indians did. Make them from a piece of birch bark if you can find one on the ground, or use the pattern on page 22 of this book to make them from cardboard. These goggles will also help during a blizzard, and you'll find that while regular sunglasses often frost over, these won't.

Mittens are better

The best way to keep your hands warm is to wear warm, waterproof mittens over a thin knitted pair. Gloves are not as warm because they don't trap as much air and they also prevent your fingers from warming each other. If your hands do get cold anyway, hold them over your head, then drop them forcefully a few times. Or take your mittens off and put your bare hands under your armpits.

Carry a big stick

If you are walking in unfamiliar territory, it's useful to carry a long pole made from a sturdy branch. You can use it to test the ground ahead to make sure it's safe to step on.

"Air trap" clothing

You can trap warmth next to your body by wearing many loose layers of clothing instead of just one or two tight layers. And if you find your coat isn't keeping you warm enough, you can stuff dry leaves inside your shirt and they will help keep you warm. The pockets of air between the leaves provide ideal places for warm air to be trapped. This is why fluffy clothes made of wool or down keep you so cosy.

The heat-making body machine

Your body is a wonderful machine. While you are outside enjoying yourself in winter, there are many things going on inside your body of which you might not be aware.

Skin – a changing coat

Your skin also works to keep you warm. When the weather's cool the blood vessels under the surface of your skin contract or get smaller. This keeps most of the warm blood deep inside the body where it's needed and away from the surface of your body where it would get cold.

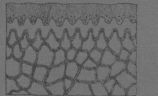 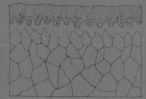

Shiver to keep warm

When you play outside for too long in winter you automatically start to shiver. Have you ever wondered why? It's simple. Shivering makes many of your muscles move and this movement warms you up. The more you move when it's cold, the warmer you become.

A hair-raising idea that no longer works

Have you ever noticed how animals and birds fluff up when they are cold? They do this so that air that has been warmed by their bodies will be trapped by their fur or feathers. At one time people had much hairier bodies than today and tiny muscles raised these hairs to trap warm air next to their skin. Today, these tiny muscles that lift each hair produce goose pimples, but we now have so little hair that this natural reaction doesn't help keep us warm.

Warm heart, cold feet

The most important parts of your body are your brain, your heart and your lungs. So, when it is cold your body naturally keeps most of your warm blood around these areas. This is why your hands and feet get cold first. They are getting less blood.

Eat to keep warm

Just like a furnace, your body produces heat by burning fuel. The fuel your body burns is food or food-storing tissues, such as fat. The colder it is the more fuel your body needs and this is why you need to eat more in the winter.

Winter Wisdom

It's great to explore the outdoors in winter but you must keep your wits about you. Here are a few tips that will help.

1. Always dress warmly before you go outside.
2. Bright colours are best for winter so you can always be seen easily.
3. Never venture onto ice unless it has been tested first by an adult.
4. Never explore unknown territory alone, and if you do go exploring, always tell someone where you are going and when you plan to be back.
5. Prevent frostbite by making faces and wiggling your fingers and toes. If it's very cold check your friend's face often for signs of frostbite (white spots on the skin). If you see signs of frostbite, gently warm the skin with your bare hands, and hurry home. Never rub the area with your hands or snow as this could break the skin.
6. If you should get lost, a plastic whistle comes in handy. Blow it at regular intervals to summon help. If you don't have a whistle shout at regular intervals.
7. If you become lost, stop walking immediately, then retrace your footsteps. If you can't find your tracks, it is foolish to use up your energy quickly as you might not be found for a few hours. So, look for a sheltered place that can be seen easily by searchers, and make a comfortable dry place to crouch on by covering the ground with evergreen branches.

HOT 'N' COLD

An Arab in summer

What do this Arab and Inuit (Eskimo) have in common? Believe it or not, they stay cool or warm in exactly the same way.

Both cultures, over thousands of years, have developed clothes that trap air. This trapped air keeps the Arab's body cool in the day yet warm at night and it keeps the Inuit warm even in an extremely frosty climate. Both their suits of clothing work a bit like those lightweight styrofoam food containers that you take on picnics. Whether in a very hot or a very cold place, the air trapped in the styrofoam keeps what's inside the same temperature as when you packed it.

Why are we telling you this? Because you can discover some useful hints for keeping warm this winter—and cool next summer, too...

The *gafiyah*, or skull cap, traps air and keeps out the scorching heat.

As protection from sunburn, the Arab drapes a triangular piece of cloth, called the *ghutyra*, over his or her skull cap. This is also good protection during fierce sandstorms.

An Arab's clothes are loose and flowing. They act like a portable tent, not only keeping the sun's heat away from the body but also letting in any desert breezes.

The favorite fabric for an Arab? Lightweight white cotton, for two cooling reasons. The white reflects the sun away from the body and cotton absorbs perspiration and dries quickly.

Desert sand is hot, so Arabs wear thick-soled leather sandals. Open shoes are much cooler than tight boots because air can get in and circulate around the toes.

An Inuit
in winter

Inuit wear two separate layers of loose-fitting clothes, as you can easily see in this illustration with a cutaway that lets you look at all the layers. Inside: an undershirt and trousers; outside: coat and trousers. These layers are ideal for trapping air close to the body and absorbing perspiration.

This Inuit woman is wearing a warm suit of caribou skins. The hollow hairs are excellent for trapping body warmth. Today, less expensive man-made materials are more in use, but they're often twice the weight of caribou skins.

Mittens, either caribou or sealskin, are usually two layers thick. Sometimes each mitt has two thumbs, so in case one side of the mitt gets wet, it can be turned inside out to be worn on the dry side.

Socks, made from a double layer of rabbit or other soft fur, help keep feet warm.

For extra insulation, Inuit sometimes put a pad of grass or moss between their socks and boots.

All Inuit wear a hood to stop heat from escaping from the top of their heads. A woman has a larger hood—the *quliktak*—that doubles as a baby pouch whether it's worn up or down.

A soft fur cap and vest plus heat from the mother's body keeps the baby warm.

A woman's coat is sometimes longer at the back than a man's because she needs to sit down more often while sewing and doing other household chores.

High caribou-fur boots keep out cold air and waterproof sealskin soles keep feet dry.

The "Mixed-Up" Window Puzzle

Through each window you can see a different time of year, but the windows are in the wrong order. Can you put them in the correct order? Early autumn is number 1. What is number 2, and so on? Put the numbers in the boxes under each window. Answers on page 128.

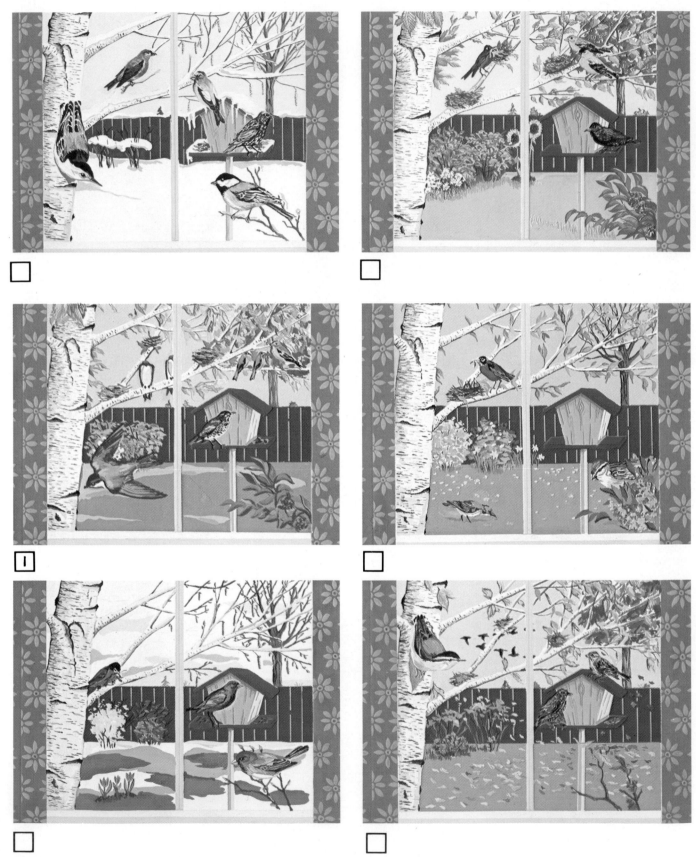

HOCKEY TIPS

One of the world's great hockey superstars is Frank Mahovlich—or the Big M—as his fans call him. Even though he's retired now, Frank scored an amazing 533 goals during his 18 years with the National Hockey League. One of Frank's most favorite memories is shooting pucks on the frozen pond near his home when he was just 12 years old. What better player than Frank to share on-and-off-the-ice hockey tips with you on the next two pages...

What makes a great hockey player like Frank Mahovlich? Most people can skate and pass a puck but a champion is someone who's worked hard and practiced until playing to win is as easy as riding a bicycle. The most important advice Frank Mahovlich gives young players is to forget about fancy shots until you've mastered the basics . . . .

Passing

Look where Frank is watching. He's able to make a good pass because his eyes are on the person he's passing to and not on the puck. Here are some more passing tips.

• Aim the puck so it goes ahead of your teammate. That way, he or she doesn't have to turn his or her head or slow down to reach the puck.

• When you watch a hockey game at an arena or on TV, you'll see that the players are out on the ice before the game starts. They're doing more than aimlessly skating—they're loosening up and practicing a few plays. Why not try warming up before your game? Skate around the rink three times one way and three times the other.

• To get the puck to a player across the ice, sweep your stick smoothly over the ice, keeping the bottom of the stick blade flat on the ice.

• If a teammate is in a better place on the ice to score than you are, pass the puck to him or her.

• Is your opponent's stick or skate blocking the way of a good pass? Get the puck up and over by tilting the stick blade up and flicking your wrist as you swing the stick forward.

• You've got to be just as ready to receive a pass as to make one. Keep your hockey stick close to the ice during the whole game so you won't miss the puck.

• Try not to pass when you're in front of your own net. Why make it easy for the other team to grab the puck and maybe even score?

Off-The-Ice Tips

Here are some things you can do even before you lace up your skates. They're guaranteed to help you play better.

• Skating is hard work. To get your legs and ankles in top shape, walk up and down stairs sideways in your bare feet. Jump rope.

• Limber up your body by standing on your toes, holding your arms over your head and stretching.

• To handle the hockey stick expertly, you need strong wrists. Here's a simple exercise to help:
You'll need:
rope 2 m/6 feet long
an old shoe
a broom handle

1. Tie one end of the rope to the shoe and the other end to the middle of the broom handle.
2. Grab the underside of the handle so your hands are 15 cm/6 inches apart.
3. Stretch your arms straight out in front of you at shoulder level. Your elbows should be pointing to the floor.
4. Roll the handle in your hands toward you so that the rope wraps around the pole and the shoe comes up. Practise the wrist roller everyday and you'll soon be able to try it with a bigger shoe tied on the rope.

Shooting

There's not much room or time to move up at net. But Frank's ready to score with the tricky backhand shot. Scoring goals is more than good luck.

● Close up to the net, try a wrist shot. The secret is to whack the puck with one forward sweep of the stick. Don't bring the stick back.

● Look at the place you're aiming to shoot—not at the puck.

● What a powerful shot! How can you tell by just looking at this illustration? See how smoothly the stick sweeps across the ice. Try this sweep shot to clear the puck away from your own end.

● As soon as you're finished your shot, skate after the puck. You should be just as ready to play and win as you were before.

Winter Fun Hockey Puzzle

So you know hockey? Test yourself on the following hockey facts, then try stumping your friends.

Q. What's the most matches played by a goal-tender without letting the other team score?
A. One hundred and three by Terry Sawchuck in his 20 seasons with the National Hockey League. He played for Detroit, Boston, Toronto, Los Angeles and New York during that time. He has also played in a record 971 games.

Q. What goaltender had the most shutouts in one season?
A. George Hainsworth of Montreal had 22 shutouts in 1928-29. This feat is even more amazing considering that the season was only 44 games long at that time, compared to today's 80-game season.

Q. Who has scored the most points in one game?
A. Darryl Sittler of the Toronto Maple Leafs scored 10 points on February 7, 1976, against the Boston Bruins. He had six goals and four assists.

Q. Who holds the season record for assists and points?
A. Wayne Gretzky of the Edmonton Oilers set season records for assists (109) and points (164) in the 1980-81 season. His average of just over two points per game is also a record! Including the playoff, his season record assist and point totals are 123 and 185.

Q. Who's the fastest skater?
A. Bobby Hull was clocked at 47.7 km ph / 29.7 miles per hour with the Chicago Black Hawks.

Q. What is the longest any team has been penalized in one season?
A. The Philadelphia Flyers in 1975-76 lost 1,980 minutes in penalties.

Q. Who has scored the most points ever?
A. Gordie Howe of the Detroit Red Wings scored 1,850 points with 1,049 assists in his National Hockey League career. That's a record!

Q. What is the longest any goalie has gone without defeat?
A. Thirty-three games, a record set by Gerry Cheevers of Boston in the 1971-72 season.

Q. What were the most goals scored in a World Championship match?
A. Canada beat Denmark on February 12, 1949 with a score of 47-0.

AMAZING HOCKEY QUIZ

Whether you're a player or cheering from the boards, it's important to know what the referee is signalling. How quickly can you match the pictures of the signals with the list below.

N

C

L

K

F

A

J

I

H

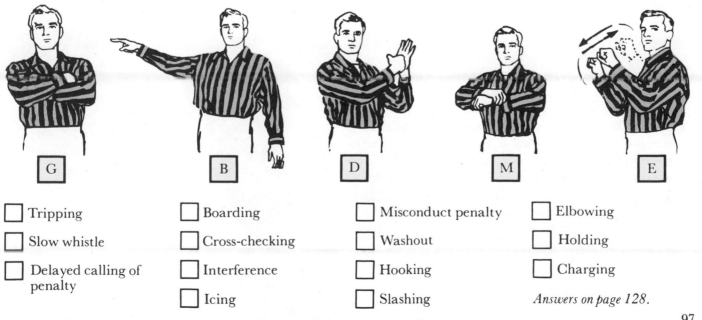

G

B

D

M

E

☐ Tripping

☐ Slow whistle

☐ Delayed calling of penalty

☐ Boarding

☐ Cross-checking

☐ Interference

☐ Icing

☐ Misconduct penalty

☐ Washout

☐ Hooking

☐ Slashing

☐ Elbowing

☐ Holding

☐ Charging

Answers on page 128.

THE BRAVE EMPEROR

The Antarctic in winter is a land of total darkness, raging blizzards and ice storms. It hardly seems the right place or the best time to raise a family, but that's just what the emperor penguin does. It has a good reason: the emperor's chick needs a long time to grow up without danger from predators. By the time winter comes again it must be fat and healthy or it will perish...

As the days in March grow shorter and winter approaches, long parades of emperor penguins begin to wander inland to their breeding grounds on the ice. April arrives before each bird has found its mate among all the thousands of look-alike emperors. And another month passes before the female lays one large greenish-white egg. By then, of course, it is completely dark and the temperature is about –50°C/–58°F. So her mate loses no time in rolling the egg onto his webbed feet and tucking it snugly under a flap of skin below his belly. That done, the female waddles off to find the sea.

But where is it? What was once open water is now solid ice. The female is exhausted and very, very hungry because she's had nothing to eat for seven or eight weeks. But she has a long journey across the ice and snow before she can fling herself into the water to feed on fish.

But what of her mate? Each parent has a special task to do if their chick is to survive, and *his* job starts now. For about another two months he'll keep the egg warm. During blizzards he'll hobble closer to other fathers for warmth, always being careful not to drop his precious egg. And there they'll stand, shoulder to shoulder, backs to the wind, balancing eggs on their feet. Only by standing very close and very still can emperors conserve their energy.

That they can survive at all is miraculous, but something even more miraculous now happens. Between 62 and 64 days after she has left, the female returns—just as the chick is hatching. The female recognizes her mate's voice and rushes straight to him, standing so close that their toes touch. Quickly she moves their newly hatched chick onto her own feet and tucks it under her warm belly. Now the reason for her incredible journey and her mate's long, cold wait becomes clear.

She's carrying about 14 kg/30 pounds of chunky fish and squid soup in her stomach, which she can feed a little at a time to her chick. Now it's her mate's turn to leave for the sea.

And what a pitiful sight he is! After standing around in the cold with nothing to eat but snow for so long, he can hardly stumble along. He has lost so much weight that his skin hangs in folds. But somehow, staggering across the ice and sliding on his belly over the snow, he manages to reach open water. What a relief it must be to fall into the cold, dark sea and feed. Fortunately, he quickly regains his strength and weight and three weeks later heads back to his mate, carrying another stomachful of food for the chick.

The two hard-working emperors feed their chick in this way until it's about six weeks old. By then it's covered in a thick gray down and can survive without their body warmth. So it joins the other babies in the colony's nursery, where it is cared for by a few adults and several immature penguins. Life for its parents is now a little easier because they don't have to take turns starving. But they do continue to take turns racing back and forth with food.

Finally, at five months old, their chick loses its baby down and grows its first waterproof feathers. Summer has arrived and the sea ice is breaking up under the colony. The young penguin travels north with the pack ice—together with thousands of other penguins—swimming, feeding and growing fat on krill.

SOME BIRD!

Top Hat 'n' Tails

There's a very good reason for the penguin's black and white suit. It makes the bird very difficult to see in the water. A predator looking down on a penguin probably won't notice its dark back against the dark depths of the sea. And a predator looking up will likely miss the penguin's light belly against the sunlit surface of the sea.

What a Shape!

The penguin can't claim the prize for the world's most graceful animal on land, but it's certainly among the most graceful in the sea. It's so well streamlined that it can even do "dolphin leaps" over and under the waves.

Wings or Flippers?

Penguins, while they are birds, stopped flying many million years ago, and their "wings" are now rigid and boardlike. They're useful, however, for flying along underwater and as paddles for tobogganing over fresh snow—a favorite penguin pastime.

Penguin Crooners
Imagine a chorus of several thousand emperor males all singing to attract their mates. The amazing thing is that the females recognize their own mate's love song.

Underwater Champ
Emperors can dive to a depth of 250 m/800 feet and hold their breath for up to 18 minutes at a time.

Winter Underwear
A penguin doesn't worry about the cold because it wears four layers of "clothes." Under its very thick skin is an even thicker layer of fat. And at the base of each waterproof feather is a tuft of down that helps trap air. It's a bit like wearing an eiderdown jacket *and* a wet suit.

Waterproof Suit
No matter how long a penguin stays underwater, its skin never gets wet. That's because its feathers overlap as tightly as fish scales.

Big Bird
The emperor penguin is the largest of all, growing to a height of 1 m/3 feet, and weighing up to 46 kg/ 100 pounds.

Odd Bird Out
The emperor penguin is the only bird in the world that begins to breed in autumn rather than the spring.

Cool Bird
How do you keep cool in summer when you're wearing a hot suit? A penguin does it by pumping extra blood into its thin skinned feet and flippers. Then it flaps its flippers to let heat escape from its body.

Br-r-r-r
Summer in the Antarctic

It all begins with tiny plants called phytoplankton. In the summer, currents warm the water so billions of these tiny plants can grow. The water starts to look a bit like green soup.

The "plant soup" is a meal for many kinds of animals: tiny, one-celled animals called zooplankton, little shrimplike creatures called krill (that you see magnified here) and, of course, fish.

The small animals are food for larger creatures such as Adelie penguins. Although these well-insulated fatties waddle clumsily on land, in the water they swim so gracefully that they catch fish and krill with ease. But life is not carefree for Adelie penguins. Before a dive, they always check carefully for signs of another, much larger hunter: the leopard seal.

While you're shivering through a winter day, animals near the South Pole are basking in bright summer sunshine. But even when it's sunny in Antarctica, it's still very cold, so you can't help but wonder why all those animals would live in such a place.

The answer is simple: food. In the summer there's plenty of it for those animals who have developed special ways to beat the cold.

The big, sharp-toothed leopard seal gets its name from its spots and, like the penguin, is protected from the cold by a "blubber suit." It lurks close to shore waiting for a group of Adelie penguins to take the plunge. Each penguin is unwilling to be first in the water, but finally one dives in. If it's unlucky it will end up in the sharp teeth of the leopard seal, but at least the rest can swim in safety.

Even the large and ferocious leopard seal isn't totally safe. Its enemy is the killer whale. Hunting in packs, killer whales can surround and attack an unwary leopard seal before it has time to realize anything is wrong.

Olde Tyme Winter

Today, not many of you have to put socks on over your leather-soled shoes to keep from slipping on the ice. And these days, we rarely have to pull a horse out of an icy pond or cut holes in the ice to rinse out the washing. But we still do a lot of the same things for fun that people all over the world did long ago.

It's a neat trick if you can do it! Skaters long ago tried the Spread Eagle skating position, too.

Snowshoeing was a much more popular sport and form of transportation years ago. Everyone—big and little—got in on the act.

Since you couldn't entertain yourself in front of the television, a great evening would be a wintry walk in the moonlight.

Frozen ponds were ice rinks, and crowds of people flocked there on fine days.

People everywhere in the world where there was ice and snow were skaters, including these Russian gentlemen.

It's a far cry from the boot skate of today, but tie on a couple of old blades like this and you could move pretty well on the ice.

Skaters certainly kept warm in olden days. But if you fell down in all those clothes, imagine trying to get up.

Sleighs were everywhere during winter long ago. Children harnessed theirs to anything that would move.

In grand cities such as Paris, some of the 19th century sleighs were very stylish—as were the passengers.

Sleigh horses wore bells for a very good reason—sleighs didn't have horns. The children riding behind their goat in this picture (see them?) would have no trouble hearing this German horse if they were to meet it on the road.

Children have always had great ideas for getting places. But is the Canadian boy hitching a ride (in the old time picture on the left) as safe as he thinks he is?

107

If snowmen are fun to build, why not make a snow sculpture of your favourite pet? That's just what this Japanese girl did over 200 years ago.

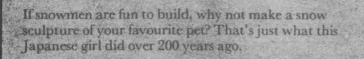

Just as cars have accidents today, horse drawn vehicles of yesteryear had their share of mishaps. This Cornelius Krieghoff painting of Quebec in the 1850s says better than we can that life in those days was a real adventure!

The "WASTE NOT, WANT NOT" Game

The two people who live in this house waste a lot of energy. For instance, the outdoor lights are blazing when one small light (or even none) would do. Look carefully at both the inside and outside of this house and see if you can spot 13 more ways to save energy.

Answers on page 128

FANTASTIC ICE CASTLES

Ice castles like the one here are easy to make. And the more you use your imagination the more fantastic they will be.

As building blocks you will need lots of different icy shapes. Egg cartons, for example, produce gumdrop shapes for decoration; plastic vegetable trays make ice slabs for soaring walls or roofs; cupcake tins and plastic funnels produce turrets; plastic bowls and yoghurt or cottage cheese containers and jelly molds make crazy towers.
Water expands as it freezes, so never use glass molds. They may shatter.

1. Fill all your molds with water and leave them outside to freeze overnight—the temperature must be 0°C/32°F or lower. Add drops of food coloring to the water if you want a colored castle.

2. Choose the best place for your castle—flat and not too exposed to direct sunlight.

3. Unmold your ice shapes by dipping them into a bucket of warm water. Do this outside. It's best to wear wool gloves with plastic bags over them to protect your hands.

4. The most important part of your castle it its foundation. Prepare the ground for this foundation by adding a little water to the snow to make some slush. Press some blocks into the slush and hold them there for a few seconds until they freeze to the ground. Then repeat the process using slush to hold the rest of the blocks together.

5. Once your foundation is solid, experiment with creating twisting turrets and towers, crazy staircases, windows, perhaps even a drawbridge. If you do not want to cement the upper walls together with more slush, try using a plastic plant sprayer filled with warm water to freeze-join your castle together.

6. For really impressive spires try freeze-joining icicles to the top of your castle.

Penguins are good jumpers and can leap 2.5 m/8 feet out of the water onto the icy shore.

One sure way to avoid the flu is to go to a very cold place, like the South Pole. It's so cold there that germs can't survive long enough to make people sick.

Even a fish can freeze if it swims for long in icy waters. But not the Trematomus which lives in the Antarctic regions. It has a special ingredient in its blood called glycoprotein that keeps it from freezing.

The pintail duck has been clocked at 82 km ph /51 miles per hour as it flies south to its winter home in central Europe.

What color is snow? If you said white, you're wrong! Each snow crystal is as clear as ice and therefore acts like a prism to break light into all the colors of the rainbow. But unfortunately, our eyes can't see this and so to us snow looks white.

Summer snowstorms in Europe and North America? It happened in 1816, and temperatures that year were so cold it was nicknamed the "Year Without Summer." The reason? The year before, a volcano exploded thousands of miles away in Indonesia. It let off lots of volcano dust that circled earth reflecting back into space the sun's heat that we should have got.

The husky—of Arctic sled dog fame—has wide, fur-padded feet that are perfect for moving through snow. But occasionally, when sea ice becomes flooded, large ice splinters will form. When this happens, sled dogs are fitted with tie-on canvas boots.

Did you know that bright colors absorb more heat than white? That's why most Arctic flowers are pink, yellow or purple. That's one way to survive in a climate where there's not much heat to absorb.

Budding flowers in January on the snowy North American prairies? In certain areas a southwest wind called the Chinook blows in. This wind is so warm that snow turns to water in its path, animals come out of hibernation and flowers may even bloom.

Icebergs in the desert? It's not as odd as it sounds. Scientists are experimenting with towing icebergs from the Antarctic to Australia to provide a good supply of fresh water. There's just one problem yet to solve: most icebergs melt before they reach their destination.

Sorry. Rudolph the Reindeer couldn't possibly have a red nose. Why? Reindeer rely on their noses to smell out small plants under the snow, so their muzzles are covered with fur to prevent frostbite. Besides wearing these built-in nose muffs, reindeer grow their own version of woolly socks— bristly hairs that protect their foot pads from snow and ice.

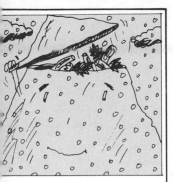

Two hundred thousand years ago Antarctica had a warm climate. We know this because fossil remains, leaves and wood have been found under the ice cap.

A pink walrus is a warm walrus. Blood vessels in its blubber that are normally kept closed in the cold to prevent loss of body heat open up when it is warm so blood rushes to the skin.

Willow trees in the northern tundra areas of the world grow to only 15 cm/ 6 inches high. Severe winters, strong winds and very short growing seasons stunt their growth.

The next time you see red snow you *can* believe your eyes. What you're looking at are millions of tiny plants called algae that grow in clumps in the snow.

115

MATCH THE SNOWFLAKE

Ever heard that no two snowflakes are the same? Some snowflake experts now say this may not be necessarily so. Out of the billions of flakes that fall in the world each year, there might be at least two that are alike. Chances are you'll never see them, but out of these 30 flakes you should be able to pick out the two that are identical.

Answer on page 128

117

Who's Under the Snow?

There's more going on in this winter scene than these two sparrows feeding. Not all animals sleep the winter away or travel to warmer weather. Some are leading busy lives under the snow. That's because the snow's such a good insulator that it's much warmer underneath than up top.

Turn the page for a peek into this cozy world under a blanket of snow . . .

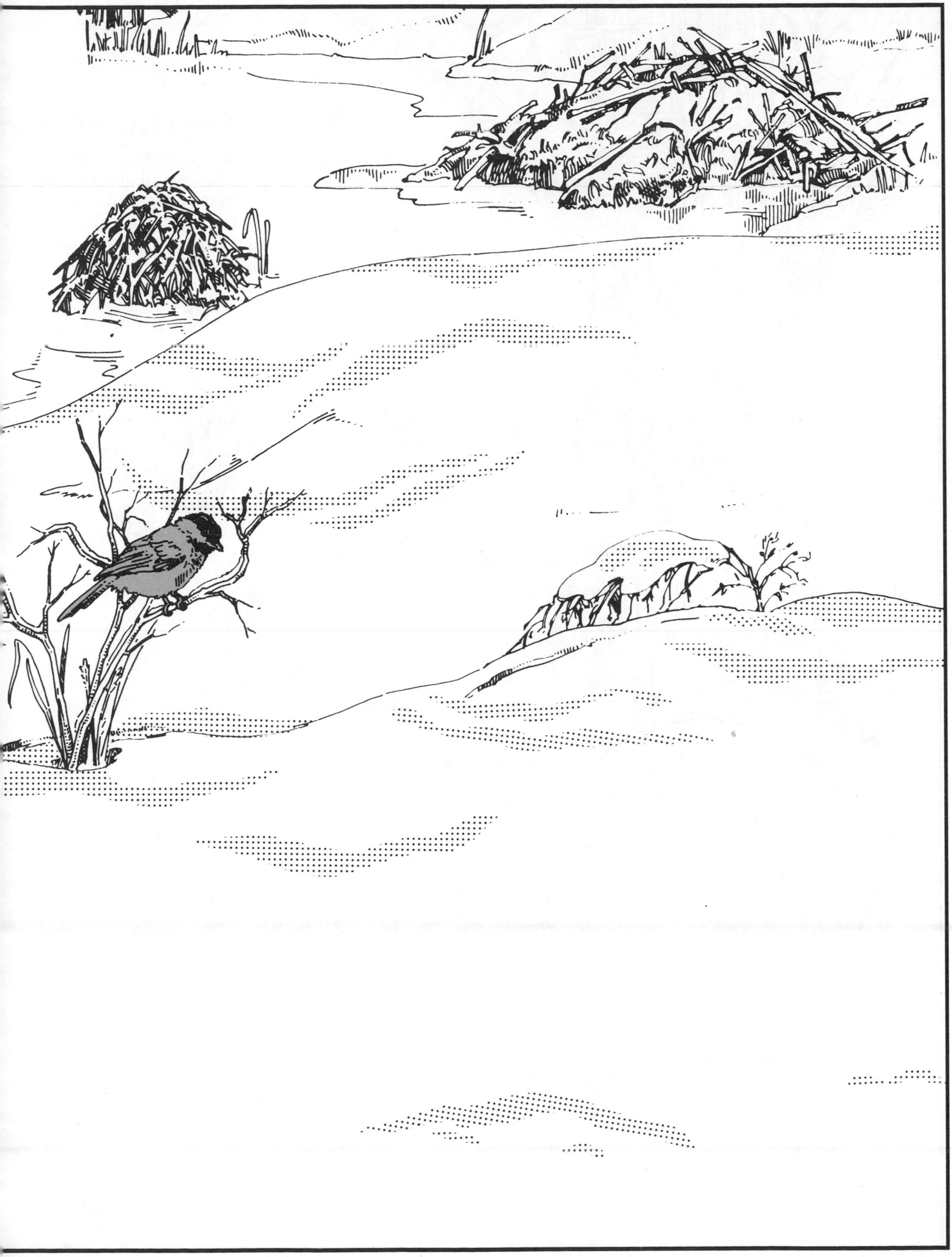

Who's Under the Snow?

There's more going on in this winter scene than these two sparrows feeding. Not all animals sleep the winter away or travel to warmer weather. Some are leading busy lives under the snow. That's because the snow is such a good insulator that it's much warmer underneath than up top.

1. Ruffed Grouse
These birds have an unusual way of keeping warm. They simply fold their wings and dive headfirst into a snowbank. Once under the snow, they can make small tunnels to a food supply of plants.

2. Scorpionfly
Crowds of these tiny, dark insects are ready to come out on the snow during a warm spell.

3. Snowfleas
Pepper sprinkled on the snow? No—these are fleas called springtails named for their habit of suddenly "springing" forward in the snow. You can see them in late winter on the south side of trees.

4. Collared Lemming
Lemmings have bigger feet in winter than at other times—the third and fourth claws on their forefeet grow longer. This helps lemmings tunnel through snowbanks to build nests.

5. Masked Shrew
Whether beneath the snow or above, this tiny creature is busy all winter hunting for grasses, grains and insects to feed on.

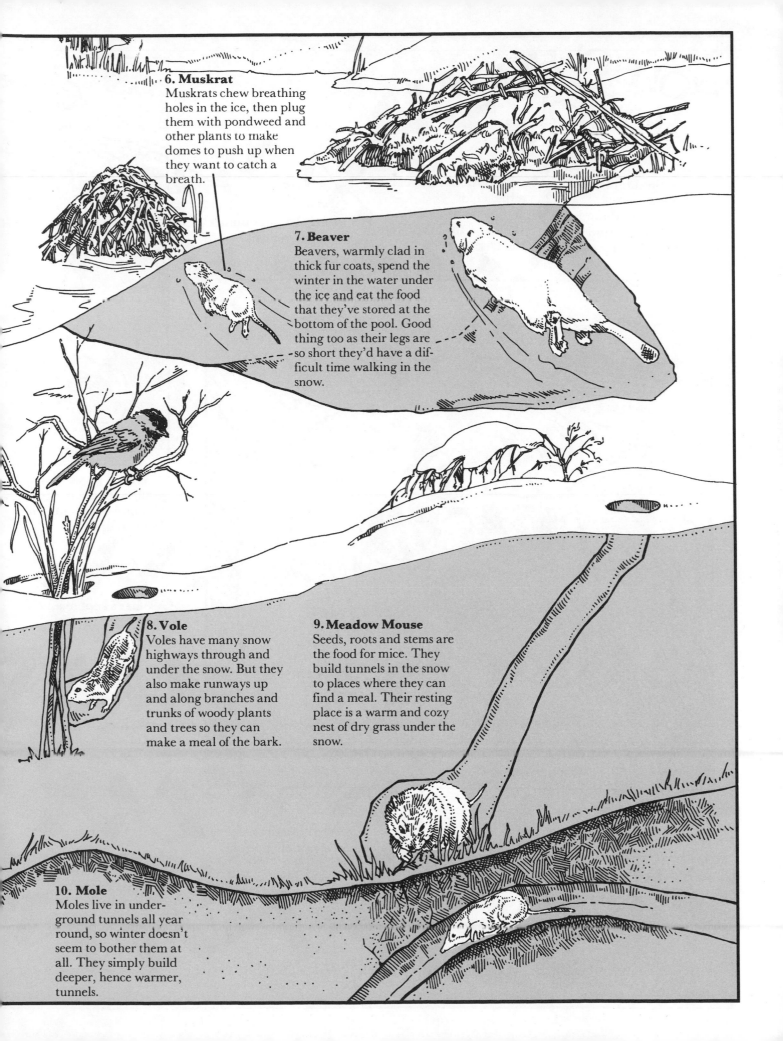

6. Muskrat
Muskrats chew breathing holes in the ice, then plug them with pondweed and other plants to make domes to push up when they want to catch a breath.

7. Beaver
Beavers, warmly clad in thick fur coats, spend the winter in the water under the ice and eat the food that they've stored at the bottom of the pool. Good thing too as their legs are so short they'd have a difficult time walking in the snow.

8. Vole
Voles have many snow highways through and under the snow. But they also make runways up and along branches and trunks of woody plants and trees so they can make a meal of the bark.

9. Meadow Mouse
Seeds, roots and stems are the food for mice. They build tunnels in the snow to places where they can find a meal. Their resting place is a warm and cozy nest of dry grass under the snow.

10. Mole
Moles live in underground tunnels all year round, so winter doesn't seem to bother them at all. They simply build deeper, hence warmer, tunnels.

HO! HO! HO! HO! HO! HO!

Q. Why is a dog dressed warmer in summer than in winter?
A. Because in winter he wears a fur coat and in the summer he wears a fur coat and pants.

Q. What's the difference between a bus driver and a bad cold?
A. One knows all the stops and the other stops the nose.

Q. What has more feet in winter than in summer?
A. A skating rink.

Q. What's worse than a giraffe with a sore throat?
A. A hippopotamus with chapped lips.

Q. What's kept in an air-conditioned vault?
A. Cold cash.

Q. What sheet can't be folded?
A. A sheet of ice.

Q. Why is a goose like an icicle?
A. Because it grows down.

Q. What is steam.
A. Cold water going crazy with the heat.

Q. What usually has a bald top, a big bottom and jumps?
A. A ski slope.

Q. What goes out black and comes in white?
A. A black cow in a snowstorm.

CHAPPED LIPS.

Q. What's the difference between the North Pole and the South Pole?
A. All the difference in the world.

Q. When will a net hold water?
A. When the water's frozen.

Q. Why do birds fly south in winter?
A. Because it's too far to walk.

Q. Why does the air seem fresher in winter?
A. Because it's kept on ice.

Q. Did anyone laugh when you fell on the ice?
A. No, but the ice made some awful cracks.

Q. What is plowed but never planted?
A. Snow.

Q. What is black and white and red all over?
A. A blushing penguin.

Q. What stays hot no matter how cold it gets?
A. Pepper.

Q. What's the hardest thing about learning to skate?
A. The ice.

Q. What moves faster, hot or cold?
A. Hot. Everybody can catch cold.

Q. What is visible only in winter?
A. Your breath.

Q. What's an eavesdropper?
A. An icicle.

THIS WALKING SOUTH IN THE WINTER IS FOR THE BIRDS!

123

BE A WINTER DETECTIVE

See how many of the things in this imaginary winter scene you can match up with the clues below. Write the numbers opposite the clues.

Answers on page 128

☐ A mud-lined Robin's nest, built high in the trees

☐ Yellow or red-shafted flickers leave holes like these

☐ A catbird nest hidden in low bushes

☐ Raccoon tracks, showing heel and toe marks

☐ Long slashes on a tree made by the rare pileated woodpecker

☐ Nest of a red-winged or tricolored blackbird, found in reeds

☐ Twigs cut cleanly by a hungry rabbit

☐ Squirrel nest, made of branches with dead leaves still attached

☐ The starling, in its speckled brown winter coat

☐ This young tree may die from being gnawed by mice

☐ Cat tracks

☐ Pecking rings in a tree left by a sapsucker

☐ Long tracks made by the hind legs of a rabbit

☐ The screech owl

How do you rate?
Perfect score—super
10 to 13 clues identified—great
7 to 10 clues identified—good
Under 7 clues identified—better luck next time

BE A "SIGNS OF SPRING" DETECTIVE

Spring seems to happen suddenly, but it's really a very long process. It begins in February and ends in June—depending on where you live. In winter things appear to die, but may not—as spring proves. But you have to be a really good detective to recognize the very first signs of this season. See if you can spot the 12 signs of spring in this imaginary scene. Then ask your friends if they can find them...

Answers on page 128

How do you rate as a
Spring Sign Detective?
9-12 Excellent
6-8 Good
4-6 Fair
Less than 4—Take
another look

ANSWERS

Answers to the Crossword Puzzle on page 29

Across

1. scarf 4. nap 6. Mites 9. otter 10. air 11. merry 13. sleds 16. hockey tips 18. win 20. blizzard 22. tracks 24. fire 25. nest 27. rescue 29. tunnels 30. summer

Down

1. snow 2. Antarctic 3. farm 4. near 5. play 6. Mars 7. tyme 8. sits 12. reindeer 14. low 15. den 16. hibernate 17. skates 19. ice cream 21. animals 23. skier 26. tent 28. club

Answers to Snow Sleuth Quiz on pages 30-31

1. The warmed roof caused the snow to melt. As the drops of water reached the cold eaves, contact with colder air caused them to freeze again. 2. The snow melted off the roof because this house is poorly insulated and heat can escape through the roof. The snow on the jutting eaves stayed cold and did not melt. 3. No, it's a motorbike. 4. The driveway with steep banks of snow along its edges was plowed. The other driveway with less even edges, lower sides and piles of snow just beyond its edges was blown clear by a snow blower. 5. These icicles were formed by snow melting off the hood of a warm, moving car. The wind blew the melted snowdrops back where they contacted cold air and froze to form crooked icicles. 6. The air underneath manhole covers warms up more quickly than the cold sidewalk or road. 7. Someone just like you! Can you make the same tracks? Or make up some new patterns? 8. The builders obviously forgot to insulate along the rafters of this house because heat is seeping out here and causing the snow to melt in strips. 9. Look at the weathervane on the top of the house and then look at the rest of the scene. The wind was blowing from the west and trapped more snow on the west side of the hedge, trees and roofs than on the other sides. 10. The snow on the bottom of this pile is older and has picked up a lot of dirt and pollution. The top snow is quite fresh, however, and hasn't had time to get dirty. 11. A car was parked here before the first snowfall and has just been moved. 12. The snow stayed on this roof because the garage is not heated.

Answers to Winter Word Search on page 36

Owls are amazing birds. They can see better than people in both the daylight and the dark, and they can hear a mouse rustle eight city blocks away.

Answers to Be a Tracking Detective on pages 78-79

1. False 2. False 3. False 4. False 5. True 6. True 7. True 8. False 9. True 10. False

Answers to the Mixed-Up Window Puzzle on page 92

3, 6, 1, 5, 4, 2

Answers to the Hockey Puzzle on page 97

A. *Tripping*: Tripping another player with your stick, knee, foot, arm, hand or elbow.

B. *Slow Whistle*: A linesman may hold off blowing his whistle if there's an offside only if there's no damage done to the defending team's position. But if there is damage, the whistle is blown.

C. *Delayed Calling of Penalty*: Only two players of the same team can be in the penalty box at the same time. Therefore, the next player on the team to get a penalty must wait until one of the two players is out of the box to start his own penalty.

D. *Boarding*: Shoving, charging or tripping another player into the boards.

E. *Cross-checking*: Cross-checking another player with both your hands on your stick and no part of your stick touching the ice.

F. *Interference*: Blocking a player who doesn't have the puck.

G. *Icing*: The puck shot up the ice from behind the red center line across the opposing team's goal line is first touched by an opposing player. A face-off is called.

H. *Misconduct Penalty*: Using abusive language or signs to a referee or other official.

I. *Washout*: If the referee makes this signal it means the goal doesn't count, but if a linesman makes the signal it means no icing.

J. *Hooking*: Trying to stop a player from skating away by using your hockey stick as a hook.

K. *Slashing*: Swinging your stick at your opponent.

L. *Elbowing*: Trying to stop or block a player with your elbow.

M. *Holding*: Grabbing or holding onto a player or his stick.

N. *Charging*: Running or jumping on another player.

Answers to the "Waste Not, Want Not" Game on pages 110-111

1. Open windows let the heat out. 2. Open curtains at night also let the heat out. 3. Dripping taps waste water. 4. Leaving lights on in empty rooms is wasteful. 5. The refrigerator door should be kept shut when possible. 6. The TV and radio are on at the same time. 7. An open door lets the heat out. 8. If possible, recycle bottles and newspapers. 9. The heat from the stove burner is being wasted heating such a small pot. 10. Large fires are bad because most of the heat goes up the chimney. 11. The snow on the roof has melted, causing icicles, because the roof is not properly insulated. 12. Unused rooms should have the heat turned off and the doors shut. 13. Full baths waste hot water. Try a half-full bath or a short shower. short shower.

Answers to the Snowflake Puzzle on pages 116-117

The snowflake that's second from the right in the top row is identical to the snowflake that's second from the left in the bottom row.

Answers to Be A Winter Detective on pages 124-125

9. Robin's nest 8. Flicker hole 1. Catbird's nest 4. Raccoon tracks 2. Pileated woodpecker hole 6. Blackbird nest 5. Twigs bitten off by rabbits 11. Squirrel's nest 13. Starling 12. Mice gnawed this small tree 3. A cat's tracks 11. The sapsucker's holes 7. Rabbit tracks 14. The screech owl

Answers to Be A "Signs of Spring" Detective on pages 126-127

1. Mud patches are beginning to show. 2. Ice on the stream is melting. 3. A skunk cabbage is growing in a small mud patch near the stream. The plant makes heat as it grows, which melts the surrounding snow. 4. The crow calling from the tree is one of the first birds to establish its territory in the spring. 5. The red willow near the stream is starting to bud. 6. One of the starlings is carrying nesting material. 7. Geese are flying north to their nesting grounds. 8. The horned lark flying over the stream is one of the first birds to return from its wintering grounds. 9. Tiny springtails can be seen in the snow in the foreground. 10. The long icicles hanging from the fallen tree show that the nights are still cold enough to keep icicles frozen, but the days are getting warmer and more snow is melting to add to the icicles' length. 11. The elm tree branch to the right is starting to bud. 12. Sap is being collected in a bucket from the maple tree.

Credits

pp. 8/9 Jonathan Milne, 10/11 Tony Thomas, 12/13 Tony Thomas, 14/15 Malak, 16 Jonathan Milne, 17-20 Tony Thomas, 21-28 Linda Bucholtz, 29-31 Elaine Macpherson, 30/31 adapted from the book *Snow Stumpers* by David Webster (Doubleday & Co., 1966), 32/33 Gord Oglan, 37 illustration by Ludek Pesek from *Journey to the Planets* by Peter Ryan published by Penguin Books, © Ludek Pesek, 1972, 38/39 NASA, 40/41 Mary Carrick, 42/43 Fred Bruemmer, 44 Canadian Wildlife Service, 45 Gord Oglan, 58-60 Elaine Macpherson, 61 Akira Uchiyama (Photo Researchers, Inc.), 62/63 Beth Eldridge (moose, mountain goat), Leonard Lee Rue III (red fox, hare), 64/65 Teiji Saga (Photo Researcher, Inc.) 66/67 William R. Fraser (penguin), George Calef (ptmarigan), Edgar T. Jones (snowy owl), 68 William R. Fraser, 69 Elaine Macpherson, 70-77 Mark Thurman, 78/79 Elaine Macpherson (special thanks to Jim Arnosky and his book *I Was Born in a Tree and Raised by Bees* (G.P. Putnam's Sons, 1977), 82/83 Gord Oglan, 84/85 Tony Thomas, 86-91 Olena Kassian, 92 Elaine Macpherson, 93-95 photos by Graphic Artists, 96 Gord Oglan, 97 *Ice Hockey Rules in Pictures*, edited by Robert Scharff (Grosset & Dunlop, New York, 1967), 98-103 Elaine Macpherson, 104-108 Metro Toronto Library, 109 Cornelius Krieghoff *The Upset Sleigh*, late 1850's from the collection of The Hon. K.R. and Mrs. Thomson, reprinted from the book *Krieghoff* by J. Russell Harper (University of Toronto Press, Toronto, Ontario, 1979), 110/111 Clive Dobson, 112 Tony Thomas, 114/115 Gord Oglan, 116/117 *Snow Crystals* by W.A. Bentley and W.J. Humphreys (Dover Publications, New York; General Publishing, Don Mills, Ont.), 118-121 Elaine Macpherson, 122/123 Gord Oglan, 124-127 Elaine Macpherson

Cover

Lynda Cooper

IF YOU LIKED THIS BOOK, LOOK FOR OWL'S SUMMER FUN BOOK.

IT'S HOT!